FALLEN

A STUDY OF THE DEVIL AND HIS DEMONS

by Dr. Randy T. Johnson

with contributions by:

Roger Allen	Shawna Johnson
Noble Baird	Josh Lahring
Chris Cain	Lorna Lyman
John Carter	Wes McCullough
Trevor Cole	Mark O'Connor
Caleb Combs	Ken Perry
Isaiah Combs	Phil Piasecki
Jayson Combs	Ryan Story
Jen Combs	Holly Wells
Donna Fox	Kyle Wendel
Debbie Gabbara	Tommy Youngquist
John Hubbard	

Copyright © 2017 The River Church

All rights reserved. No part of this book may be reproduced or transmitted in any form or by any means, electronic or mechanical, including photocopying, recording or by any information storage and retrieval system, without the written permission of The River Church. Inquiries should be sent to the publisher.

First Edition, May 2017

Published by:
The River Church
8393 E. Holly Rd.
Holly, MI 48442

Scriptures are taken from the Bible,
English Standard Version (ESV)

THE RIVER CHURCH

Printed in the United States of America

CONTENTS

WEEK 1: HIS FALL

- Study Guide **9**
- Devotion 1: Pride Before the Fall **15**
- Devotion 2: Warning: Falling Objects **17**
- Devotion 3: Ya' Missed it **19**
- Devotion 4: Pride Bad, Humility Good **21**
- Devotion 5: Flawless to Lawless **23**
- Devotion 6: Skywalker to Skydiver **27**

WEEK 2: HIS MISSION

- Study Guide **31**
- Devotion 1: Fight **37**
- Devotion 2: Lying "Lion" **39**
- Devotion 3: Up or Down **41**
- Devotion 4: The Destruction of Destraction **43**
- Devotion 5: Kingdom Seeker **47**
- Devotion 6: The Hunt **49**

WEEK 3: HIS ANGELS

- Study Guide **53**
- Devotion 1: How then Shall We Live **61**
- Devotion 2: Reel is too Real **63**
- Devotion 3: Even Demons Believe **65**
- Devotion 4: Holy, Holy, Holy **67**
- Devotion 5: Toby or not Toby **69**
- Devotion 6: Know God, No Fear **71**

WEEK 4: HIS PREACHERS

- Study Guide..**75**
- Devotion 1: Know the Book..**81**
- Devotion 2: "O be Careful Little..."...**83**
- Devotion 3: Transformed?..**85**
- Devotion 4: Hole in Won...**87**
- Devotion 5: False Teachers..**89**
- Devotion 6: Falling Star Wars...**91**

WEEK 5: HIS END

- Study Guide..**95**
- Devotion 1: Satan's End..**101**
- Devotion 2: The Bubble..**105**
- Devotion 3: The End...**107**
- Devotion 4: Ding Dong the Witch is Dead and Rosebud was his Sled..**109**
- Devotion 5: Not Today Satan..**111**
- Devotion 6: Lake of Fire...**113**

PREFACE

Fallen is a study from Bible passages concerning the devil and demons. No one should dabble with the Ouija board, fortune tellers, black magic, séances, spirits, and the demonic world. However, that does not mean the believer needs to walk in fear or as having been defeated. 1 John 4:4 clearly says, **"Little children, you are from God and have overcome them, for he who is in you is greater than he who is in the world."** Romans 8:31 adds, **"What then shall we say to these things? If God is for us, who can be against us?"** The Holy Spirit dwells within the children of God. He protects and brings victory. Remember Paul's words in 2 Timothy 1:7, **"For God gave us a spirit not of fear but of power and love and self-control."**

Fallen consists of five study guides for personal or group discussion and thirty devotions to help you understand the devil's fall, mission, angels, preachers, and end.

> Spoiler alert: Revelation 20:10 says, **"And the devil who had deceived them was thrown into the lake of fire and sulfur where the beast and the false prophet were, and they will be tormented day and night forever and ever."**

01 / DR. RANDY T. JOHNSON, GROWTH PASTOR

HIS FALL

His Fall

There are some 40 names for the devil in Scripture. The most common and well known are Beelzebub, Evil One, Lucifer, and Satan. The devil was created like all other angels, exalted to a high position, became discontented, aspired to be God, and was cast from Heaven.

The two major passages that describe the fall of the devil are Ezekiel 28 and Isaiah 14. Both readings start by talking about an actual king that morph into a dual reference. C.C. Ryrie writes, "Ezekiel saw the work and activity of Satan, whom the King of Tyre was emulating in so many ways."

What do you think caused the fall of the devil? __SIN__
__UNRIGHTEOUSNESS - filled w/ VIOLENCE__
__Pride__

> Ezekiel 28:12-17
> "Son of man, raise a lamentation over the king of Tyre, and say to him, Thus says the Lord God: 'You were the signet of perfection, full of wisdom and perfect in beauty. 13 You were in Eden, the garden of God; every precious stone was your covering, sardius, topaz, and diamond, beryl, onyx, and jasper, sapphire, emerald, and carbuncle; and crafted in gold were your settings and your engravings. On the day that you were created they were prepared. 14 You were an anointed guardian cherub. I placed you; you were on the holy mountain of God; in the midst of the stones of fire you walked. 15 You were blameless in your ways from the day you were created, till unrighteousness was found in you. 16 In the abundance of your trade you were filled with violence in your midst, and you sinned; so I cast you as a profane thing from the mountain of God, and I destroyed you, O guardian cherub, from the midst

His Fall

> of the stones of fire. 17 Your heart was proud because of your beauty; you corrupted your wisdom for the sake of your splendor. I cast you to the ground; I exposed you before kings, to feast their eyes on you.'"

Describe the devil from verse 12. *PERFECTION - FULL OF WISDOM - BEAUTY*

According to verses 13 and 15, was the devil infinite (did he always exist)? *NO*

Explain verse 14. *ONE OF THE PRIVILEGED ANGELS - SURROUNDING GODS THRONE. SATAN HAD GREAT FREEDOM.*

What was the cause of the devil's fall (verses 15-17)? *SIN - PRIDE*

What was the result of the devil's sin? *SEPARATED FROM GOD*

> 1 Timothy 3:6
> "He must not be a recent convert, or he may become puffed up with conceit and fall into the condemnation of the devil."

His Fall

In 1 Timothy 3 Paul gives Timothy the qualifications for an elder (Pastor) and in the process references what caused the fall of the devil. What was it? _PUFFED UP - PRIDE_

> Proverbs 16:18
> *"Pride goes before destruction, and a haughty spirit before a fall."*

What does this verse mean? _PRIDE WILL RUIN YOU_

Have you seen this in others or ever experienced it yourself?

> Isaiah 14:12-15
> *"How you are fallen from heaven,*
>   *O Day Star, son of Dawn!*
> *How you are cut down to the ground,*
>   *you who laid the nations low!*
> *13 You said in your heart,*
>   *'I will ascend to heaven;*
> *above the stars of God*
>   *I will set my throne on high;*
>   *I will sit on the mount of assembly*
>   *in the far reaches of the north;*
> *14 I will ascend above the heights of the clouds;*
>   *I will make myself like the Most High.'*

> 15 But you are brought down to Sheol,
> to the far reaches of the pit."

What name is given for the devil in verse 12? _____
Day Star Son of Dawn _____

What name is given for God in verse 14? _Most High_

Summarize the five "I wills" in this section. _Pride_

The devil did not want to "settle" for "just" being God. He wanted to be higher than God. Obviously, pride was the problem. It can also be a struggle for all of us. Without careful attention, it is our natural de-"fault."

The key to being careful with pride
is not to think less of yourself,
but to think of yourself less.

> Proverbs 16:5
> "Everyone who is arrogant in heart is an abomination to the Lord; be assured, he will not go unpunished."
>
> Psalm 10:4
> "In the pride of his face the wicked does not seek him; all his thoughts are, 'There is no God.'"
>
> Romans 12:16
> "Live in harmony with one another. Do not be haughty, but associate with the lowly. Never be wise in your own sight."

His Fall

1 Corinthians 13:4

"Love is patient and kind; love does not envy or boast; it is not arrogant."

The devil was in a privileged position and fell. What can we learn from this? __Power Grabs?__

"Satan, the leader or dictator of devils, is the opposite, not of God, but of Michael." C. S. Lewis

If that is true, what is the opposite of God? __DEATH/HATE__
__LIAR__

His Fall / Devotion 1

PRIDE BEFORE THE FALL

Isaiah Combs / *Worship Leader & Young Adults Director*

The fall of Satan was because of pride. Satan believed himself to be greater or could be higher than God. His pride caused him to be cast out of Heaven. 1 Timothy 3:6 says, ***"He must not be a recent convert, or he may become puffed up with conceit and fall into the condemnation of the devil."*** The devil still uses that same pride to cause believers to fall.

I remember as a teenager being super proud of myself the first time I beat my dad in shooting pool (billiards). He usually would beat me pretty easily. He became superb at pool when he was a kid. His father bought him a pool table, not so he could enjoy it, but so he could teach my dad to get excellent and then hustle people at the bar. So needless to say, my dad became superb at pool and did not lose his skill as he got older. He would try and teach me tools and tricks of the game, but I was not an excellent listener and never got very good. But I did have one motivating factor. I hate to lose. I refused to let my dad beat me over and over again. I would go down in the basement after school or when my dad was not home and practice. My hate of losing drove me to practice more and more. My pool game was slowing getting better. I was also building up the courage to challenge the master (my dad) again.

One night at dinner I felt confident enough to challenge my dad to a game. He agreed, and after we had eaten, we went down to the pool table. I racked the balls because the loser always racks. He broke and began probably the worst game he ever played in his life. I, on the other hand, was on fire (even a blind squirrel finds a nut every once in awhile). I made it quick and beat my dad for the first time.

I began to gloat and tell my dad his reign of terror was over. I had become the best pool player in the house. He asked me if I wanted to play again after I had finished my winner's speech that I may have or not had written on some note cards and had been preparing for a month (I had a lot of free time apparently). So my dad racked the balls (because HE LOST). He then seemed to have a laser-like focus the likes of which I had never seen him play with before. He beat me the next five games easily, and I went back to my old job of racking the balls and learning.

The Bible has a funny way of telling you sometimes exactly what you need to hear.

> Proverbs 16:18 says, *"Pride goes before destruction, and a haughty spirit before a fall."*

I let my pride get the best of me. I won one time and thought I had arrived. Then my pride quickly was smashed and crushed into tiny pieces (and used as pool stick chalk).

I know this is a funny story of pride. But this is us in our lives. I believe the devil loves to convince us that we do not need God and we can do it on our own. We begin to think of ourselves as self-sufficient and capable of doing it all on our own. We get prideful, and quickly we are knocked off our high horse. I am not saying being proud of accomplishments are bad. But the key is giving glory to God for that achievement. All good things are from the Lord.

> Remember: *"Every good and perfect gift is from above"* (James 1:17).

His Fall / Devotion 2

WARNING: FALLING OBJECTS

Phil Piasecki / *Worship Leader*

When we think of the devil, we envision a crazy looking monster with horns and a pitchfork. I am sure we have all seen the drawings, he always has a tail, and sometimes is even wearing a cape! However, these pictures we have in our heads are very inaccurate. We see in Scripture that Satan was a beautiful and brilliant angel. He began his existence in Heaven with Christ, only to be cast out due to his pride. We find the following account in Scripture:

> *"How you are fallen from heaven, O Day Star, son of Dawn! How you are cut down to the ground, you who laid the nations low! You said in your heart, 'I will ascend to heaven; above the stars of God I will set my throne on high; I will sit on the mount of assembly in the far reaches of the north; I will ascend above the heights of the clouds; I will make myself like the Most High.' But you are brought down to Sheol, to the far reaches of the pit. Those who see you will stare at you and ponder over you"* (Isaiah 14:12-16).

We see here that Satan desired to make himself like Christ, his ambition was only to make himself greater. This desire leads to him being cast out of Heaven and to be removed from the very presence of God. When I read this account in Scripture, it boggles my mind. Satan was one of God's angels, living in the perfection of Heaven, in the presence of God! Why would he desire anything else? However, after thinking more about this, I realized that this is something each of us does every single day. All of us behave in ways that say to God "we want to be our own gods." We all have times in our lives where we are so prideful in who we are, that we lose complete sight of who God is. We are warned against this type of behavior in Proverbs:

> *"Pride goes before destruction, and a haughty spirit before a fall"* (Proverbs 16:18).

I believe that the word "fall" was specifically used for a reason in this Proverb. It points us back to the fall of Satan and the fall of Adam and Eve. The fall of Satan can be directly tied to his pride, and pride in our lives can lead to our fall in the same way. We have the daily opportunity to live in awe of the glory of Christ, to truly have His presence felt in our lives, yet so many of us substitute that in place of our glory. Living a life in search of our pride and glory cannot even begin to compare to the alternative. Christ wants us to fellowship with Him daily. We were created to spend our lives dwelling in Christ! We cannot view the fall of Satan as just a historical tale; we must consider it as a warning for our lives. Do not let pride or your glory cause you to miss out on the life God created you to experience.

His Fall / Devotion 3

YA' MISSED IT

Ryan Story / *Student Pastor*

Take some time today to read Luke 10, specifically the sending of the 72 and the return of the 72. This is a great portion of Scripture where Jesus instructs His followers to go into towns and preach the Gospel. It is amazing to read about "ordinary people" who had the faith to follow Jesus and live out what He commands. However, there is a tragedy in these verses. When the 72 returned, they almost seemed to miss something. There is a scary correlation between the disciples and Satan.

> Luke 10:17-20 reads:
> *"The seventy-two returned with joy, saying, 'Lord, even the demons are subject to us in your name!' And he said to them, 'I saw Satan fall like lightning from heaven. Behold, I have given you authority to tread on serpents and scorpions, and over all the power of the enemy, and nothing shall hurt you. Nevertheless, do not rejoice in this, that the spirits are subject to you, but rejoice that your names are written in heaven.'"*

When the disciples came back to Jesus to report, they were full of joy to tell Jesus what they had just done. Imagine how excited they were to tell Jesus that because of His name they were able to do miraculous deeds! And even Jesus agrees saying He saw Satan fall from the sky like a bolt of lightning. Jesus seeing Satan fall is an attribute that Jesus has, since Jesus is God, the ability to see past, present, and future. For all you deep Bible people, feel free to read about the idea of prophetic perfect. So when Jesus sees Satan fall, He is seeing Himself cast him out of Heaven, his fall because the disciples were beginning to work for the Kingdom of God and

Satan's final fall. Jesus does a good job to affirm the disciples with saying that He is, in fact, their power, but then Jesus drops a truth bomb, "Do not rejoice in this (that they have power over the enemy) that the spirits are subject to you." Jesus turns around and brings the 72 back to reality in those few words. Jesus then reminds them to make sure they rejoice because their names are written in Heaven.

Many times in our Christian walk we struggle with a thing called pride. Pride can manifest itself in hundreds of ways. Some pride is self-centered while other forms are self-loathing. Pride can look like a person who is always craving to be in control or a person who cannot cease from talking about what they have accomplished. Pride is the scariest sin because it is the exact reason Satan got cast from Heaven. While Jesus most likely was proud of the 72 people He sent out because of their work, they quickly tainted the whole "living for Jesus thing" by showing that they were more proud of the work they did, than the reason why they were working. No Christ follower should be doing ministry so they look good, they should do it because they are motivated by *"your name is written in Heaven."*

So where has Jesus sent you? For some of us it is our schools or workplaces. Are you working for Jesus to look good and get recognition from others? Or are you working because He sent you in, to preach the Good News of Christ?

His Fall / Devotion 4

PRIDE BAD; HUMILITY GOOD

Wes McCullough / *Production Director*

No one is good at everything, but everyone is good at something. Therefore, every person is at risk of becoming prideful. You should be proud of yourself, giving thanks to God in the process, but be careful, the Bible has some strong words about pride.

We have all heard the familiar phrase, "Pride comes before the fall." Not surprisingly, these wise words come from Proverbs. No one in history experienced this principle so literally and more severely than Satan. He was once on the holy mountain of God and was described as the Day Star, perfect in beauty and blameless, but he became filled with pride and desired to overthrow God, so God cast him out of Heaven.

Let us look at the ancient Israelites and learn from their repeated failure at humility. For forty years they wandered in the desert while God stripped them of their pride. Only when they embraced humility and a reliance on their Heavenly Provider did they settle into the homeland God had promised. It is too bad they could not remember this lesson. Their struggle with the pride/humility concept continually led to war, exile, and captivity. Like before, it took a long time for them to learn a simple concept- pride bad, humility good.

If pride is on one end of the spectrum humility is on the other end. Satan's refusal to humble himself cost him everything. The Bible is very clear on how God feels about pride and humility:

> *"For you save a humble people, but the haughty eyes you bring down."* (Psalm 18:27)
>
> *"The Lord lifts up the humble; he casts the wicked to the ground."* (Psalm 147:6)
>
> *"Whoever exalts himself will be humbled, and whoever humbles himself will be exalted."* (Matthew 23:12)
>
> *"Humble yourselves before the Lord, and he will exalt you."* (James 4:10)

These few examples give us clear instructions on how we should conduct ourselves if we seek to please God and desire His favor in our lives.

God is the Creator, the Provider, the Sustainer and we have nothing, are nothing without Him.

> *"Clothe yourselves, all of you, with humility toward one another, for God opposes the proud but gives grace to the humble"* (1 Peter 5:5).

His Fall / Devotion 5

FLAWLESS TO LAWLESS

John Carter / *Director of Finance & HR*

The concept of the fall is real as the title expresses, going from a flawless state to lawlessness. In Genesis 1 we see that God created all things and God saw that it was very good. We were made flawless, but guess who else was made and created a flawless being, the devil. Yeah, shocking to consider that Satan, the devil, Lucifer, was once a perfect creature made by God. So the question is, "What went wrong?"

Ezekiel 28:12-15 gives a description of the King of Tyre that spiritually represents a description of the devil. One of the key clues to this is provided with the description in verses 13-14.

> *"Thus says the Lord GOD: "You were the signet of perfection, full of wisdom and perfect in beauty. 13 You were in Eden, the garden of God; every precious stone was your covering, sardius, topaz, and diamond, beryl, onyx, and jasper, sapphire, emerald, and carbuncle; and crafted in gold were your settings and your engravings. On the day that you were created they were prepared. 14 You were an anointed guardian cherub. I placed you; you were on the holy mountain of God; in the midst of the stones of fire you walked. 15 You were blameless in your ways from the day you were created, till unrighteousness was found in you."*

These are obviously not descriptions fitting to any earthly human king. The subject of who the King of Tyre is involved a much deeper study than available in this context. Some believe he was possessed by the devil; others say he is the devil. I want to focus on fundamental concepts that describe what happened with the devil.

Let's focus on what went wrong with the devil.

Verse 15 of Ezekiel states "you were blameless (or flawless) from the day you were created, till unrighteousness (or sin) was found in you." As you continue in the Scripture to verse 17, you can see why sin was found in him. *"Your heart was proud because of your beauty; you corrupted your wisdom for the sake of your splendor. I cast you to the ground; I exposed you before kings, to feast their eyes on you."*

"Your heart was proud because of your beauty." The devil's first mistake was the sin of pride. God's response to sin can be seen as a depiction of the fall when He says, *"I cast you to the ground."* We see here that pride was a big issue involved in the devil's fall. You might be thinking that this is an interesting topic, but how does this relate to me? You might say things like, "I am not the devil. I know he is the "bad guy." What does this event have anything to do with me?"

As I was studying this topic, I felt like I was being led to 1 John 3. Verse 4 says, *"Everyone who makes a practice of sinning also practices lawlessness. Sin is lawlessness."* When we sin, we are lawless. The passage continues in verses 7-10, we are given a warning not to be deceived. *"Little children, let no one deceive you. Whoever practices righteousness is righteous, as he is righteous. 8 Whoever makes a practice of sinning is of the devil, for the devil has been sinning from the beginning. The reason the Son of God appeared was to destroy the works of the devil. 9 No one born of God makes a practice of sinning, for God's seed abides in him, and he cannot keep on sinning because*

he has been born of God. 10 By this it is evident who are the children of God, and who are the children of the devil: whoever does not practice righteousness is not of God, nor is the one who does not love his brother."

The story of the devil is not that different than the fall of the human race, as recorded in Genesis 3. We were made flawless, lived in a flawless environment, but our pride made us think we knew better than God. In fact, we thought we could be God, the same as the devil thought.

So to the question, why does understanding the fall matter? Well, the fall matters because it helps us to understand the history of how we went wrong. If we cannot identify the problem, then we cannot see an effective solution to the problem.

As we saw at the end of verse 8, the reason Jesus Christ came was to destroy the works of the devil. This means that we have hope! Yes, we gave up flawlessness for lawlessness. How dumb are we? So let us learn from it and not let our pride keep us from recognizing who Jesus Christ is and that He came to give us a flawless solution. What will you choose? A Flawless Jesus Christ or your lawless pride?

The very first verse of 1 John Chapter 3 says this, **"See what kind of love the Father has given to us, that we should be called children of God; and so we are."** This is the hope part of the Gospel, the part that helps us understand the flawless gift the Father sent in his Son. It seems crazy when we look back at the fall that someone would give up perfection to live out their lawless prideful living. Why on earth did Adam and Eve trade out paradise for disobedience? Seems totally crazy right? The fact is God has given us another Perfect, Flawless solution to our first mistake. His name is Jesus Christ, yet there are some who instead of humbling themselves and recognizing who Christ is, they would choose to live in lawlessness. The fall is important because it is a history lesson, and as the saying of Edmund Burke goes, "Those who do not know history are destined to repeat it."

His Fall / Devotion 6

SKYWALKER TO SKYDIVER

Noble Baird / *Community Center Director*

I am a huge Star Wars fan. If you ask anyone who knows me or has been to my house, Star Wars has been a huge part of my childhood. So, fair warning, I am about to sound like a massive nerd in these next paragraphs, but stay with me as we use this remarkable cinematic example to parallel with Satan. When *Episode 1 - The Phantom Menace* came out, to say I was excited is an understatement! Finally, I could see a Star Wars movie in theaters, just like my dad had seen the originals. The movie focuses on little Anakin Skywalker and the beginning of his journey with the force. For those of you who have not seen the Star Wars saga, fair warning — Spoiler Alert! As the movies progress through to Episode 3, we see this innocent child become the evilest and most powerful villain in the *Star Wars Universe*, Darth Vader.

In Ezekiel 28:14-17, Ezekiel is referencing the King of Tyre; however; as we read over the passage there is a dual meaning here. Not only is Ezekiel speaking of the king, but he is also referencing back to Satan's fall. He writes starting in verse 14, **"You were an anointed guardian cherub. I placed you; you were on the holy mountain of God; in the midst of the stones of fire you walked. You were blameless in your ways from the day you were created, till unrighteousness was found in you. In the abundance of your trade you were filled with violence in your midst, and you sinned; so I cast you as a profane thing from the mountain of God, and I destroyed you, O guardian cherub, from the midst of the stones of fire. Your heart was proud because of your beauty; you corrupted your wisdom for the sake of your splendor. I cast you to the ground."** Here, Ezekiel paints a picture of the fall of

Satan. He states Satan's status amongst the other angels as a guardian cherub. Yet, Satan was overcome with unrighteousness and therefore, as Ezekiel tells us, God cast Satan to the ground (the earth).

Anakin, when found by Obi-Wan Kenobi and Qui-Gon Jinn, was filled with potential. He had been created to do incredible things with the force and ultimately to save the galaxy from the Sith. In the same way, Satan was created as a guardian cherub. God had created him as one of His most beloved and most trusted. However, just like Anakin, Satan was corrupted. Unrighteousness, violence, and pride were found in him. Therefore, because of the sin that had overcome him, Satan was cast out of Heaven, stripped of his status and stature amongst the angels, and the relationship between him and God was severed.

As Anakin grew older the anger, violence, unrighteousness, and pride in his life began to overcome him as a young Jedi. This darkness slowly spread to every facet of his being, and he became the fallen Jedi, Darth Vader. In the same way, Satan was overcome by these things which led to his fall as an angel. As we continue this study on Satan, I challenge you to examine your life. We see through Scripture and especially in the life of Satan, how one can be overcome by sin. Daily, we all struggle with sin, however when we get to the point where sin becomes who we are and our life, that once innocent child which God created for great things can become fallen and destroyed by the world.

02 / *PASTOR JAYSON COMBS, FAMILY PASTOR*

HIS MISSION

His Mission

One of my brothers is the Pastor of a Church in Columbus, Ohio. I have had the privilege of speaking at his Church several times. I will never forget the first bit of advice my brother gave me when venturing into an Ohio pulpit as a Michigan native. He said, "Jay, do not joke about it…it never goes well." Of course, he was referring to the ongoing feud between those who live in the state of Michigan and those who live in the state of Ohio. My brother explained that because the competition runs so deep, some people may stop listening if they feel you have something against their Ohio State Buckeyes. Every time I speak in Ohio, I continue to hold my tongue about Ohio State University, even though I get dealt my fair share of comments and jokes as a Pastor from Michigan.

Look at the list below, can you name the chief opponent of each item?

Alabama –
Tweety Bird – *Sylvester*
Zombies – *light*
Superman – *Crypton*
Apple (Computers) – *Devil*
God – *devil*

Do you think you give the devil too much credit? If so how?
Use him as an excuse for doing wrong.

Do you think you can take the devil too lightly? Explain.
Yes – involve yourself in things that are questionable – turn into something big.

31

If the devil had a mission statement, what would it say?

Keep us so busy with good things – even church things that we are not available for the real things of God.

Using the following verses, fill in the blanks with words that describe Satan.

> John 8:44
> "You are of your father the devil, and your will is to do your father's desires. He was a murderer from the beginning, and does not stand in the truth, because there is no truth in him. When he lies, he speaks out of his own character, for he is a liar and the <u>father of lies</u>."

> 1 Corinthians 7:5b
> "So that Satan may not tempt you because of your lack of self-control."

> John 12:31
> "Now is the judgment of this world; now will the ruler of this world be cast out."

> Peter 5:8
> "Be sober-minded; be watchful. Your adversary the devil prowls around like a roaring lion, <u>seeking someone</u> <u>to devour</u>."

> Revelation 20:10
> "And the devil who had <u>deceived them</u> was thrown into the lake of fire and sulfur where the beast and the false prophet were, and they will be tormented day and night forever and ever."

His Mission

> John 10:10
> "The thief comes only to steal and kill and destroy. I came that they may have life and have it abundantly."

_____
_____
_____

According to the following verses, how did Satan attack Jesus?

_____
_____
_____

> Matthew 2:14-16
> "And he rose and took the child and his mother by night and departed to Egypt and remained there until the death of Herod. This was to fulfill what the Lord had spoken by the prophet, 'Out of Egypt I called my son.' Then Herod, when he saw that he had been tricked by the wise men, became furious, and he sent and killed all the male children in Bethlehem and in all that region who were two years old or under, according to the time that he had ascertained from the wise men."

> Matthew 4:8-9
> "Again, the devil took him to a very high mountain and showed him all the kingdoms of the world and their glory. And he said to him, 'All these I will give you, if you will fall down and worship me.'"

> Luke 22:3
> "Then Satan entered into Judas called Iscariot, who was of the number of the twelve."

His Mission

> Matthew 12:14
> *"But the Pharisees went out and conspired against him, how to destroy him."*

Read Matthew 4:8-9 again. What did Satan want from Jesus?
To Worship Him _____
_____
_____

The word 'devil' is not another name for Satan; it is a word that describes him. The meaning of the word devil (diabolos) is to slander and accuse. John MacArthur put it this way, "The term rendered devil takes this opposition to the level of a malicious enemy who slanders and attacks."

Knowing this, what do you think Satan wants to do to you? (Read Matthew 13:19 for help) _MAKE US HIS_____
_____
_____
_____

"As the masters of the spiritual life have believed, there may be times in our pilgrimage when Satan engages in blackmailing us. We have secretly given in to sin. He whispers that we have failed; we are unworthy. He will keep our secret — so long as we keep it a secret too, and hide or disguise it. No one else must be told."
Sinclair Ferguson

In these verses, how are we told to deal with Satan?
_____
_____
_____

1 Peter 5:8-9

"Be sober-minded; be watchful. Your adversary the devil prowls around like a roaring lion, seeking someone to devour. Resist him, firm in your faith, knowing that the same kinds of suffering are being experienced by your brotherhood throughout the world."

Ephesians 6:11, 16

"Put on the whole armor of God, that you may be able to stand against the schemes of the devil."

"In all circumstances take up the shield of faith, with which you can extinguish all the flaming darts of the evil one."

James 4:7

"Submit yourselves therefore to God. Resist the devil, and he will flee from you."

Matthew 26:41

"Watch and pray that you may not enter into temptation. The spirit indeed is willing, but the flesh is weak."

Giving Satan too much credit causes us to be afraid of him. It leads us to believe we cannot overcome his attacks and deception. The Bible, however, tells us that we have strength through Christ to overcome the evil one. It tells us to stand against the darts of the devil. But the Bible also warns us to walk carefully, not as fools but as wise, redeeming the time because the days are evil (Ephesians 5:15-16). Taking Satan too lightly can put us in situations where we walk into his traps. Satan is evil, and he wants to kill, steal, and destroy our lives. He is the prince of this world and can bring pain and hurt to our lives if we do not trust and follow what God has for us.

What are some practical things that you can do this week to stand against the devil? _Be aware of what is going on around you._

His Mission / Devotion 1

F I G H T

Donna Fox / *Assistant to the Growth Pastor*

Have you ever had an important task assigned to you, or self-imposed? This is called a "mission." For instance: "It is my mission to help my children do well in school" or "It is my mission to find a solution to this problem."

God's fallen angel, Satan, or the devil, had a mission. His goal was to steer Christ off course during his time on Earth, to prevent Him from His end goal. Thankfully Jesus fulfilled His mission in spite of Satan! (John 19:30). Jesus overcame the devil several times, including His birth (Herod was going to kill all baby boys), at His temptation in the wilderness (Satan said "worship me"), and by ultimately going to the cross on our behalf.

When Satan did not succeed with Christ, he came after Christ's followers or would-be-followers. He causes a man not to believe, and therefore not to be saved (Luke 8:12). He destroys our faith in God. He camouflages the truth and poses as a true believer and teacher of the truth (1 Timothy 4:1-2) that leads us astray. His ultimate goal is to destroy the church.

But the good news is that in these 2000 plus years, Satan has not succeeded in destroying the church! We need to be vigilant in our study of God's Word, to align it with what we hear and do. We need to pray **"Get behind me, Satan,"** as Jesus says in Matthew 16:23. We need to **"Put on the whole armor of God, that you may be able to stand against the schemes of the devil"** (Ephesians 6:11).

We need to constantly be aware of him and his demons' presence all around us. Resist him. Fight against him. Pray for protection from him. If we crack the door open, he will swing it open wide and get ahold of us.

When I was in the choir, myself and another choir member would struggle with a sore throat, or waking up not feeling well. We kept telling each other to "not let the devil win." We would persevere and attend practice or attend church and sing to the best of our ability. Over and over we would say to each other how blessed WE were by resisting the temptation to stay home, and instead, coming to sing. We did not let the devil win!

Do you recognize his devious schemes? Are you praying "get behind me Satan?" Are you resisting his falsehoods and moving forward with God's truths firmly in the forefront of your mind? If not, make a decision today to FIGHT! You (and God) will prevail!

His Mission / Devotion 2

LYING "LION"

Phil Piasecki / *Worship Leader*

My wife loves the zoo. Our first couple years of marriage she always would throw out the idea of getting a membership so we could frequently go. I always resisted, typically using the argument that we did not have any kids to take so that a membership would be pointless. Now that we have our daughter Molly, I foresee a lot more zoo trips in our future. It is pretty fascinating to see those animals roaming around in their different habitats. Most of the animals look so friendly from afar; we often perceive them as house cats or dogs just larger in size. The danger in this is we do not fully grasp just how vicious each one of them can be. Each year we hear horror stories of people falling into habitats and being attacked in some way. As friendly as those animals may look, we all fully understand the danger that they present. When I see these animals walking about, I cannot help but think of the warning Scripture gives us in 1 Peter.

> *"Be sober-minded; be watchful. Your adversary the devil prowls around like a roaring lion, seeking someone to devour"* (1 Peter 5:8).

The mission of the devil is to destroy each and every life that he can. This verse warns us that he is always on the prowl looking for someone that he can destroy. However, how does he accomplish this mission? The devil finds ways to make sin look enticing to us, and he makes it seem like it will be harmless to us. If we all could see just how destructive sin was going to be to our lives, I am sure many of us would do a much better job of staying away from it.

As cute and cuddly as those animals at the zoo look, we all know that we would most likely die if we went into the habitat where they live. However, we fail to recognize the same danger in our life when it comes to sin. When we think back to the original sin of Adam and Eve, the serpent made eating the fruit from the tree as enticing as he could. He made false promises to Eve, successfully convincing her to disobey God. This is why we always need to be watchful, making sure we are aware of ways that Satan is trying to tempt us. He will try and disguise his temptation, and he will try and make it seem as harmful as possible. I have the privilege to lead worship some weeks at our Tuesday Night Recovery Gathering. I know every single person who attends Recovery would agree that they never thought beginning to use would have been as damaging to them as it has been. Most people do not sin thinking "this is going to destroy me, but I do not care." We think we can dabble in sin, and that we will come away from it unscathed. When we think this way, the enemy has us right where he wants us. Instead, let us understand the immense danger of sin, and always be on the lookout for how Satan is trying to attack our lives. Jesus Christ has given us His power to fight against all temptation, let's not be devoured by the enemy.

His Mission / Devotion 3

U P O R D O W N

Pastor Ryan Story / *Student Pastor*

Imagine your life is a ladder. Which way do you choose to go? We live in a society that tells us to climb to the top. Be your boss. Be the very best that no one ever was. Never stop working toward getting to that next rung. We live in a world that puts emphasis on making something of yourself. We live in a world that says "make yourself successful" and become the master of your domain. That kind of mentality reminds me of someone:

> *"How you are fallen from heaven, O Day Star, son of Dawn! How you are cut down to the ground, you who laid the nations low! You said in your heart, 'I will ascend to heaven; above the stars of God. I will set my throne on high; I will sit on the mount of assembly in the far reaches of the north; I will ascend above the heights of the clouds; I will make myself like the Most High'"* (Isaiah 14:12-14).

Those are the words that Satan says. The Book of Isaiah captures an insightful look into the persona of Satan. Filled with pride, conceitedness, and a longing for power, control, and authority. All Satan wanted to do was climb, climb, climb until he "ascended above the heights of the clouds."

Now there is another person that the Bible does a fantastic job showing what they did with their "life ladder."

> Philippians 2:6-8 says, *"Who, though he was in the form of God, did not count equality with God a thing to be grasped, but emptied himself, by taking the form of a servant, being born in the likeness of men. And being found in human form,*

he humbled himself by becoming obedient to the point of death, even death on a cross."

Jesus was at the very top of the ladder. He was sitting next to God during all of creation. He had holy box seats to watch everything that unfolded at the moment God said, "Let there be." Because all of creation needed rescuing, what did Jesus do? He did not argue about His place; He did not argue about His authority, He did not claim "it is not fair." He lowered Himself, again and again, and again. Jesus went from the Son of The Most High to washing feet. Went from being praised as "Holy, Holy, Holy" to being mocked and beaten. Jesus lowered Himself so we could have a chance. He lowered Himself so that we all might have a chance.

So I ask you, on the ladder of life which way are you going? Whose climbing style do you most resemble? Down, I hope?

His Mission / Devotion 4

THE DESTRUCTION OF DISTRACTION

Holly Wells / *Assistant to the Lead Pastor*

The little, non-intrusive interruptions are those often unnoticed. Maybe it is an unchecked thought out of nowhere in the middle of a prayer, to which you never return. Or what about when you check out of your day to peruse social media to "connect" with others only to get swept away and your few frivolous minutes became an hour (or more), and you feel emptier than when you logged on. Maybe constant worry and fear consume your thoughts, actions, and time, or is it relationships, food, shopping, video games, or…? What about something more obvious like sitting down to have quiet time with the Lord and every chore imaginable must be done right then otherwise the world will implode? Maybe you are getting ready to step out for the Lord in a new way, and your mind is soon taken captive by the vastness of your "disqualifications." Whether it creeps in or we seek it, unguarded distraction is a simple yet powerful tool that can reap unimaginable destruction.

It all starts in our mind. If we haphazardly accept the "innocent" thought, if we willingly accept the counterfeit reprieve, or if our shame buys the lie, the hardest part of the battle is over, and the enemy can so readily declare, "Checkmate!" We are distracted so well that we are blind to it. What have we left behind in these moments? What have we compromised in these minutes? What thoughts, ideas, or deceit have we allowed in this season, or maybe years? Distraction can seem so innocent, so trivial, and so typical that we fail to consider guarding our hearts and minds — our defenses are down. We accept various forms of distraction throughout our day that we have willingly been disarmed — we sit as prey. Our minds are frequently bombarded with tempting invitations to "look here!" and "try this!" — we look everywhere, yet focus on nothing.

The moment we are captivated by the thought, the instant we are caught up with the distraction, our eyes are no longer on the Lord — this is a very dangerous place.

> *"For the weapons of our warfare are not carnal but mighty in God for pulling down strongholds, casting down arguments and every high thing that exalts itself against the knowledge of God, bringing every thought into captivity to the obedience of Christ..."* 2 Corinthians 10:4-5

The Word of God is very clear that we are to take every thought captive to the obedience of Christ. We need to be aware of what consumes our thought-life. Do our thoughts align to what the Lord would desire? Are our thoughts anchored to Him or are they fleeting out of control in every direction? What safeguards can help us?

> *"Put on the whole armor of God, that you may be able to stand against the wiles of the devil... Stand therefore, having girded your waist of truth, having put on the breastplate of righteousness, and having shod your feet with the preparation of the gospel of peace; above all taking the shield of faith with which you will be able to quench all the fiery darts of the wicked one. And take the helmet of salvation, and the sword of the Spirit, which is the word of God; praying always with all prayer and supplication in the Spirit, being watchful to this end with all perseverance and supplication for the saints..."* Ephesians 6:11, 14-18

Each piece of the armor that God has provided is vital to fight off fiery darts, to stand steadfast and immovable, and it is essential to put on your armor! As a soldier prepares to enter the battlefield, so too must we! Notice the armor is both external — to protect the body — but also internal — to protect and gird our minds so that with the Lord, we will persevere.

> *"Finally, brethren, whatever things are true, whatever things are noble, whatever things are just, whatever things are pure, whatever things are lovely, whatever things are of good report, if there is any virtue and if there is anything praiseworthy — meditate on these things."* Philippians 4:8

Pray — ask the Lord to show you the distractions causing destruction in your life. (Psalm 139:23-24)

Seek — the Lord's truth and instruction through His Word. (2 Timothy 3:16-17)

Accept — be willing to accept what He reveals and seek accountability.

Repent — and apply His correction. (1 John 1:9)

Gird yourself — with the armor of God, take your thoughts captive, fix them on His truth.

Repeat!

His Mission / Devotion 5

KINGDOM SEEKER

Mark O'Connor / *Student Director*

"**B**e sober-minded; be watchful. Your adversary the devil prowls around like a roaring lion, seeking someone to devour." - 1 Peter 5:8

The simple statement of Satan's mission is to keep us from entering into a meaningful and lasting relationship with Jesus. This is shown in verses like 1 Peter 5:8 shown above. John 10:10 tells us he comes to steal and destroy, and he does. It is funny to me that it appears that even Satan does not fully understand the power of God. Throughout history, he has been defeated and overcome so many times, but he thinks there is still a chance of victory.

That is where we come in. We see in movies when the good guy loses a fight, and they reference that while this battle may be lost, the war is far from over. Maybe this is where Satan is. Obviously, he is on the losing end of the war, but he continues to fight, and he continues with these guerrilla-like tactics on humanity.

We battle in our spiritual lives to become more Christ-like, at least I pray that I can be continually moving in that direction. We are in a fight against a worldview that is growing ever more popular that contradicts the foundation of how Jesus calls us to live. There is no doubt that the enemy is at work in this movement. That is not to say that those who are part of these movements are satanic at heart. But the very nature of the enemy is to point us in a direction that we are acting in a manner that is pleasing to us and what we want in our selfish nature, that we would lose focus on living a life that is pleasing to God.

> Colossians 3:1-2 says, *"If then you have been raised with Christ, seek the things that are above, where Christ is, seated at the right hand of God. Set your minds on things that are above, not on things that are on earth."*

Paul instructs the Church to set our minds on things that are above and not what is happening here on earth. Jesus Himself tells us in Matthew 6 to seek first the kingdom of God. Satan will use things both big and small to distract us. It could be a little thing in your personal life. Maybe it is one of those "secret" things we do not let the rest of the world see, but are tearing our faith apart in the background. It could be an issue with a friend or family member. Or maybe it is the cumulative collection of all of the enemies' small victories in this much larger war. I do not know what he is using to distract you, but I pray that you will begin to take stock of the things that are keeping you from a meaningful relationship with Jesus.

His Mission / Devotion 6

THE HUNT

Noble Baird / *Community Center Director*

One of my father's favorite movie series of all time is *Mission Impossible*. I love how at the beginning of every movie, Ethan Hunt is given some self-destructing device, which contains the debrief on a mission for which he is requested. Whether Ethan Hunt is bouldering on the side of Dead Horse Point in Utah, sliding across the top of a speeding train, or climbing the side of the Burj Khalifa tower in Dubai; he is continually put in scenarios and missions that are seemingly impossible.

In 1 Peter 5, Peter gives us a quick and accurate description of what exactly Satan's mission is. He writes in 1 Peter 5:8-9, **"Be sober-minded; be watchful. Your adversary the devil prowls around like a roaring lion, seeking someone to devour. Resist him, firm in your faith, knowing that the same kinds of suffering are being experienced by your brotherhood throughout the world."** I love how Peter lays it out quick, easy, and in simple terms. Satan's mission is to "devour," which means he wants to destroy anyone he can. He wants to consume, overcome, control, and ultimately take with him anyone in the world. This is his mission; his mission is not to simply attack those of us who are followers of Christ, but more importantly anyone in the world who lets him have a foot in the door of their lives.

When we watch a movie like Mission Impossible, we ultimately know that the resolution at the end will have Ethan Hunt completing his mission. Along the way, yes he will face impossible odds and tasks, yet he will come out victorious. As we read in 1 Peter 5, Satan is on a mission as well. His mission is to purge and devour as many people in this world as he can, to join his cause. Yet, his resolution will not be the same as Hunt. When Christ died on the cross, He completed His mission and solidified Satan's as impossible. The veil was torn and as Paul writes in 1 Corinthians 15:55, death lost its sting and will have no victory.

So, as we move forward and continue to live one day at a time, remember Satan's mission that he has been trying to carrying out since the beginning of the world in Genesis 3. As followers of Christ, we know that he is seeking to devour anyone he can get a foothold. However, that is where our mission begins. Just as Ethan Hunt was given a debrief of his missions, Christ gave us ours when He left this world. Satan's mission is indeed impossible, but ours is not. That is why this is your mission, should you choose to accept it:

> *"Go therefore and make disciples of all nations, baptizing them in the name of the Father and of the Son and of the Holy Spirit, teaching them to observe all that I have commanded you. And behold, I am with you always, to the end of the age"* (Matthew 28:19-20).

03 / *JEN COMBS, WIFE OF LEAD PASTOR JOSH COMBS*

HIS
ANGELS

His Angels

Demons. Unclean Spirits. Fallen Angels. Rulers of Darkness. Evil Spirits. All words the Bible uses to describe Satan's Henchmen. Whew...what a heavy subject. What was I thinking signing up for this lesson? I do not watch scary movies; I avoid any conversations dealing with ghosts, demons, hauntings or any other supernatural things...because frankly, I know demons are real, and it just gives me the heebie-jeebies. Now here I am downloading sermons and reading books on all such topics. Learning SO much of how Satan uses them in everyday life. But let us start with some basics and get everyone on the same page before we get into some heavy material.

Some Basics

1. What are demons? Read Jude 1:6 and Revelation 12:3-4.

_____

_____

_____

2. Where did demons begin? Read Revelation 12:7-9 and Colossians 1:16. _____

_____

We learn about a great war in Heaven where Satan and his angels were cast out of _____ and onto the

_____.

Who created them? _____

Demons have been around since before Adam and Eve (Satan was in the garden, right?).

3. Where do they reside currently?
   a. _____ Luke 8:26-39; Genesis 3

His Angels

b. _____ Luke 8:26-39
c. _____ 2 Peter 2:4

4. Do demons believe in Jesus? Mark 1:34; James 2:19; Acts 19:15
_____
_____
_____

Now that you know this crazy fact, what is the difference between you and a demon? Read Romans 10:9. _____
_____
_____
_____

Demons believe in Jesus. And there are certainly plenty of people here on Earth that believe in Jesus. There is a difference between believing in Him and making Him Lord of your life. When you make Him Lord you repent, you turn from wickedness, give Him complete control of your life, and pursue holiness. So do you just believe like the demons? Or have you believed, repented, made Him Lord, and are pursuing holiness?

5. Does Jesus have authority over demons? Read Mark 1:32-34; Ephesians 1:19-21; Matthew 8:31-32; Luke 4:31-37; Luke 11:14; Mark 9:25; Matthew 17:18; Mark 16:9. _____
_____
_____
_____

When you were born, you were born into Satan's dominion. The Bible says that Satan is the prince of this world (2 Corinthians 4:4; John 12:31; Matthew 14:30). You were born into bondage, into sin and captive to him. Satan knows he has this hold on you from when you were just an infant. He goes to war over your soul from the moment you were conceived. He cannot do this alone, so he enlists his army of demons to help. In 1 Peter 5:8, **"Your adversary the devil prowls around like a roaring lion, seeking someone to devour."**

What are some ways the devil and his angels devour our lives?

_____
_____
_____
_____

Can I tell you that they are not as overt of ways as you think they are? Satan does not always use neon lights when he is trying to win our souls. He uses things that we think are innocent or that do not really mean anything. Ever read the horoscope section in the newspaper? Or go to a psychic reading just because you thought it was fake and would be fun to do? What about having your palm read because, "right, what do all those lines really mean?" How about the Ouija board when you were a kid and swore your friend was the one moving it? Ever go to a haunted house hoping to see something? Tarot Cards? Tea Leaves? Demonic movies?

_____
_____
_____

These are all VERY real ways that Satan and his demons move to work in your life. Anything to try and convince you that God does not possess all the power (Which we know is false. He is the Almighty.). Ephesians 6:12 plainly spells it out for us, **"For we do not wrestle against flesh and blood, but against the rulers, against the authorities, against the cosmic powers over this present darkness, against the spiritual forces of the evil in the**

heavenly places." If you are a believer, Satan uses all sorts of ways to oppress us, to hamper our growth in Scripture, to stunt our walk with the Lord and to distract us. If I can, I warn you to flee such things. Do not let his angels get a foothold in your life. Do not make light of such things. If you are not a believer, be warned because Satan's angels are always looking for a place to take up residence. We see multiple instances where people are possessed by demons in the Scripture. If the Holy Spirit does not reside in you this is always a possibility.

This subject is very personal to me. I knew at a young age that this stuff was real and to not tamper with it. It was not until I was older had I realized what an effect it had on my family. You see my grandmother (who I am very close with) grew up in a home where she was the tenth child. Not only was she the tenth child, but her father was shot as an officer on duty a month to the day before she was born. Can you even imagine growing up in a household like this? Your mother is in the middle of grieving, having to give birth a month later, tending to nine other children. Such devastation. I remember her telling me that when she was born her mother said she was born with a "veil" over her face. This "veil" meant that as she grew she would be able to "see things." When this gift never came, it was expressed to her that this was quite a disappointment and that something was wrong with her. Her mother used to go to psychic readings and believed in all such things. I do not know if this started before or after her husband died. But alas it was still something with which they tampered. I remember her telling me that her house was haunted growing up. They always told her that it was her deceased grandfather making racket upstairs and walking around. You see in her family they have all struggled with alcoholism, womanizing, severe depression, suicides, and nervous breakdowns. These are just some of the effects of being involved in occult practices. When my grandma was in her forties she had a nervous breakdown. She went to counseling in a mental institution to try and combat all of her symptoms. But no earthly doctor or psychologist could help her. It was not until ten years later when she and my grandpa started going to a little church in Waterford that they both gave their lives to Jesus. She was freed. You see only the Great Physician, The Almighty Counselor, could bring my grandmother out of the darkness and into His marvelous light. Once Jesus had a hold of her life there was not room for these demons to occupy. I called my mom and asked her if after my grandma was saved if the depression and breakdowns got better. She said, "Absolutely, so much better." You see there was a war for my grandma's soul, even though she may not have involved herself with such practices. Numbers 14:18 says, *"...visiting the iniquity of the fathers on the children, to the third and fourth generation."* There are generational effects of such sin. But praise the Lord my grandma was delivered.

Remember in the beginning when we talked about being born into Satan's dominion? Jesus gives us the opportunity to be delivered out of the chains and bondage of Satan. The definition of deliver says to bring and hand over to the proper recipient or address. My grandma when she was 50 years old was delivered to her rightful owner, Jesus. Colossians 1:13 says, *"He has _____ us from the _____ of _____ and _____ us to the kingdom of His beloved Son."*

There is power in the name of Jesus. James says that the demons believe and tremble. What are we to fear? 2 Timothy 1:7 says, *"For God gave us a spirit NOT of fear but of power and love and self-control."* We need to know we are in a spiritual battle continually, but we do not fear. Demons fear us because they know the ending. They know that God and His people prevail. They cringe at our prayers and service to Jesus Christ.

So what are ways that we can fight in this battle? Ephesians 6:13-18.

1. Verse 14a _____
_____
_____

2. Verse 14b _____
_____
_____

3. Verse 15 _____
_____
_____

4. Verse 16 _____
_____
_____

5. Verse 17 _____
_____
_____

6. Verse 18 _____
_____
_____

"One of Satan's most deceptive and powerful ways of defeating us is to get us to believe a lie. And the biggest lie is that there are no consequences to our own doing. Satan will give you whatever you ask for if it will lead you where he ultimately wants you."
-Charles Stanley

His Angels / Devotion 1

HOW THEN SHALL WE LIVE

Chris Cain / *Women's Ministry Director*

Are you at that point yet? Half-way through this book and thinking, "Is this *devilish* talk over yet? Make it stop already!" Like, can these demons just not go away? The Bible calls fallen angels - devils, demons, evil, and unclean spirits. They are supernatural, invisible, angelic, spirits. They are power hungry and love corrupting us humans to separate from God. Did God actually create THIS?

Are you fearful of demons? Should you be? John MacArthur writes, "There has always been a battleground between God and His truth and the devil and his lies. And that battleground is clearly drawn in Scripture and the fight goes on constantly. God calls to people through the truth and Satan with his demons tries to lure people away from truth with his hellish lies."

The thought of writing about demons was somewhat daunting to me, maybe a little scary. As I spent more and more time reading about them, you could say my fear factor was on the rise. But you know what scares me the most? Knowing that demons want people to be lured away from the Truth. That is what scares me.

Retreat. Drawback. No way. I am going to fight. I am filled with the Holy Spirit and armed with Truth. Ephesians 6:10-12 says,

> *"Finally, be strong in the Lord and in the strength of his might. Put on the whole armor of God, that you may be able to stand against the schemes of the devil. For we do not wrestle against flesh and blood, but against the rulers, against the authorities,*

> *against the cosmic powers over this present darkness, against the spiritual forces of evil in the heavenly places."*

Will you armor up with me? Will you battle? The Greek word *'dunamis'* is used about 120 times in the New Testament and means strength, ability, or power. You might recognize that we get our English words *'dynamite'* and *'dynamic'* from it. We are not living our Christian life in our power, but in God's and it is a miraculous and marvelous power. An explosion of power!

If you want to battle, you will fight with Truth. For those of you who have read a few of these "devotions" and say, "Eh, this is not a Bible Study, this is not deep enough," then maybe it is time to put in some sweat equity, pick up your Bible, and read the rest of Ephesians six and answer: Who wrote it and to whom? Where do you see Jesus in the passage? Why is it part of Scripture? How then shall you live?

I know how I will live. I am going to armor up! Do not let those demons lure you away from Truth.

His Angels / Devotion 2

REEL IS TOO REAL

Phil Piasecki / *Worship Leader*

The Grand Blanc location of the River Church currently meets at the Trillium movie theater each Sunday. Meeting at this site has some impressive benefits, but also has some downfalls. One of the issues we run into is the type of movies that are being advertised any given Sunday. We commonly have to hide the cardboard movie advertisements because of their content. It seems like every other month there is a new movie about demons/demon possession coming out, and of course, it has a terrifying cardboard advertisement to go with it. Obsession with demons is so prevalent in the United States, and it is no more evident than in Hollywood. They keep making those types of movies because people continue to see them. I think people are willing to open up to the demonic realm because they do not realize how real it is. It is so important that Christians understand that spiritual warfare is a very real thing.

> Ephesians 6:11-13 says, *"Put on the whole armor of God, that you may be able to stand against the schemes of the devil. For we do not wrestle against flesh and blood, but against the rulers, against the authorities, against the cosmic powers over this present darkness, against the spiritual forces of evil in the heavenly places. Therefore take up the whole armor of God, that you may be able to withstand in the evil day, and having done all, to stand firm."*

The Scriptures warn us here about the very real danger that we face each and every day as believers. The devil is not alone in his quest to destroy each and every one of us; he has an army roaming the earth looking for any opportunity to attack Christ's followers. This is why it is so important that we guard ourselves with the Armor of God! We are fighting against cosmic powers and spiritual forces of evil; we cannot survive that attack on our own. We need to look to Christ daily for our strength and protection. At the same time, we need to be wise about what we open our lives up to on a daily basis. My brother is currently a missionary in the Middle East, and the stories he has told me about the demon possession he has seen over there are harrowing. These people look for power anywhere they can find it, often calling on spirits from ancient temples, looking for something to strengthen them. Since these people are not believers, they do not have the Holy Spirit in their lives to protect them, and this leads to common occurrences of demonic possession. As believers, we have the power of the Holy Spirit to fight this spiritual war for us; we need to set our eyes on Christ and find our strength in Him. All the while, understanding that the spiritual realm is something that should not be taken lightly. We are fighting against a very real enemy, stand firm daily in the presence of Christ.

His Angels / Devotion 3

EVEN DEMONS BELIEVE

Pastor Ryan Story / Student Pastor

I have been teaching high school students the Bible for some time now. A while back I was doing a study on the Book of James with some high school boys, and we came across these verses, **"But someone will say, 'You have faith and I have works.' Show me your faith apart from your works, and I will show you my faith by my works. You believe that God is one; you do well. Even the demons believe—and shudder!"** (James 2:18-19). The room fell silent for a moment, until one of the boys said, "seriously the Book of James makes me want to stab my eye with a fork." Now I thought he was going to say his sudden conviction came from the **"I will show you my faith by my works"** part of this verse. He surprised me by asking the group a very pointed question, "If demons know that God is who He says He is, and demons believe that God is who He says He is, what makes us different?" You could hear a pin drop for a few minutes as we all processed that question. To this day, whenever I read the Book of James, I get to this part, and I ask myself a very tough question, "What makes your belief different from that of a demon?"

I have always found it a tad scary that the devil's minions probably have a better understanding of Jesus than I do. I have always wondered what kind of belief system do demons have. In Mark 5, when Jesus is casting out Legion he even tells Jesus, "What do you want with me, Jesus, Son of the Most High God?" Since Legion was many demons, I have to conclude that it was some group consensus that Jesus was, in fact, the Son of the Most High God. So demons clearly have to believe that Jesus is who Jesus said He was. Demons must know that Jesus can do all that He said He could do. Demons must believe that Jesus is the one who can set the captive free. Demons must believe that Jesus can give sight to the blind, heal the sick, and give hope to the hopeless. Demons must believe that Jesus is capable of using any person who puts their faith in Him to change the entire world in Jesus' name. If demons believe this, why do people who call themselves Christ followers struggle to believe the same thing?

So I ask, what makes your belief in God different from a demon? The key to unlocking this question is in two vital words. Faith and works. Demons had a belief that Jesus was truly Jesus, but that did not mean they were spreading the Good News around. We cannot leave our walk with God strictly on faith alone. Yes, faith is the only thing that saves us, but works are what make others see differently. Works allow us to show everyone, from the angels above to the demons in Hell, for whom we live. The thing that makes us different from a demon is the drive that we want to be the hands and feet of Jesus, not because it sounds right or we look good, but because we want the world to know who the Son of the Most High is. We want to show the world who set us free. We work to show how Jesus healed us. What makes you different than a demon? Take today to show them and God, how you are different.

His Angels / Devotion 4

HOLY, HOLY, HOLY

John Hubbard / *Worship Leader*

When you think of angels, what is the first thing that comes to mind? Is it the story of the Virgin Mary? Is it one of those Thomas Kinkade paintings that every true and holy Christian family would have at the end of their hallways? Is it the Angel of Death passing over Egypt, claiming the firstborn of every household who disobeyed the commands of God? For me, I always start humming the old hymn:

*Holy, Holy, Holy! All the saints adore Thee,
Casting down their golden crowns around the glassy sea;
cherubim and seraphim falling down before Thee,
Which wert, and art, and evermore shalt be.*

Such odd words to say and sing. This portion of the song is inspired from Revelation 4:4-6:

> *"Around the throne were twenty-four thrones, and seated on the thrones were twenty-four elders, clothed in white garments, with golden crowns on their heads. From the throne came flashes of lightning, and rumblings and peals of thunder, and before the throne were burning seven torches of fire, which are the seven spirits of God, and before the throne there was as it were a sea of glass, like crystal ... and day and night they never cease to say, 'Holy, holy, holy, is the Lord God Almighty, who was and is and is to come!'"*

I am always left in such awe when I imagine what that moment will be like to behold. At the same time, it is terrifying to think that there are angels that experienced that kind of a moment and chose to turn away from God. Later in the book of Revelation, the devil is described as a great dragon whose tail has swept down a third of the stars, a common depiction of angels. Later in the chapter, it speaks of how Satan was cast out, and all his angels with him. This passage is how we come to say that one-third of the angels turned away from God to follow the devil. They had been in that place, in Heaven experiencing the glory of God and they turned away. They saw the power of God Almighty, and they elected to praise Lucifer in His place. Were they simply deceived by Satan?

The Great Deceiver is not a title lightly given I have no doubt, but surely angels would not fall so easily into his trap. Did they see Satan's pride in themselves perhaps? They were angels just like Satan. If Satan can glorify himself, why could not they?

Many of you that read these devotions have seen something in your life that can only have been from God, be it your testimony of salvation or the transformation in the life of a family member or someone close to you who has heard the call of Jesus. You might say, just like the angels, that since you have seen God in such a real way that you could never turn away from Him. Surely nothing could come between you and Him. Before you even realize it, something that is vying for your attention will become your focus. You will start to look forward to that thing, nothing wrong with that right? Then you will tell God, "maybe tomorrow, I promise. I have got something a little more important than you; it just cannot wait. I am sure you will understand."

I guess it is not so hard to look exactly like the angels who fell.

His Angels / Devotion 5

TOBY OR NOT TOBY

Pastor Tommy Youngquist / *Children's Pastor*

I do not know about you, but I cannot handle horror movies. I will see a trailer for a new horror movie, and I will be intrigued by the mystery, but when it comes down to it, I just cannot watch it. The scariest movies are about demon possession. THEY FREAK ME OUT! When I have gone to bed after watching a scary movie, I must be covered in the blankets with only a little eye hole to see through. I will think to myself, "I am dying of heat, but these blankets will not come off because then I am exposed to whatever is out there!" The reason they scare me the most is because demons are REAL!

Now, those real demons are not going to make your head spin around your shoulders, puke uncontrollably, or go by the name of Toby, but they do want to cause you harm. They want you to fail in all that you do. They want you to be as tormented as they are. Most of the time, they appear to attack a thought you have. They know from the past what are your tendencies and fears. They know your weaknesses, and they try to exploit them. If they can get you to dishonor God in any capacity, they have temporary success.

> The Bible says in 1 John 4:1, *"Beloved, do not believe every spirit, but test the spirits to see if they are from God, for many false prophets have gone out into the world."*

There are other instances in the Gospels where Jesus cast demons out of people and restored them. Paul tells us in Ephesians that we do not **"wrestle with flesh and blood, but against cosmic powers over this present darkness, against the spiritual forces of evil in the heavenly places."** He even warns us in the same chapter to put on God's armor so we can protect ourselves from the schemes of the devil.

Believe it Church; demons are real. Here is the hope, even though they are real, God has power over them. James 2:19 says, **"You believe that God is one; you do well. Even the demons believe — and shudder!"** Demons quiver in fear at the very thought of God. The Bible also tells us that if we submit ourselves to God and resist the devil, demons will flee from us. It is very comforting to me knowing that if I believe and serve God, He will protect me from evil. Those who submit their lives to God, cannot be affected by the evil forces of the devil that want to harm us.

Demons are very real and serious business. But God has the upper hand, and so do you if you believe in God. Take comfort when you feel tormented by temptation, depression, or discontentment. Know that God is sufficient enough to supply our every need. Call on Him to help you with those feelings. Submit to God and watch the demons quiver and flee.

His Angels / Devotion 6

KNOW GOD, NO FEAR

Lorna Lyman / *Socrotary*

When I was asked to write this devotional my first thought was, I cannot do this. After I had found out I had to write about the devil and his demons, even more emotions rose up in me. I was feeling fear, anxiety, and doubt. Who do you think was putting those thoughts in my head? Our God or the devil? Certainly, it was not God.

Ephesians 6:12 says, **"For we do not wrestle against flesh and blood, but against the rulers, against the authorities, against the cosmic powers over this present darkness, against the spiritual forces of evil in the heavenly places."** I had to stop and pray. I felt at peace for a while, but by the time I got home from work the worry and fear were creeping back in. Again I prayed. I needed to give this entirely to God and not take it back. I thought I am not going to think about it right now and I tried to take my mind off it.

We need to have our spiritual foundation built on solid ground, so Satan's demons cannot sneak in and attempt to destroy what you have built. We can remain strong in our faith. The moment we let our guard down, Satan will sneak in, and we are suddenly in a spiritual battle. Matthew 7:24-27 says, **"Everyone then who hears these words of mine and does them will be like a wise man who built his house on the rock. And the rain fell, and the floods came, and the winds blew and beat on that house, but it did not fall, because it had been founded on the rock. And everyone who hears these words of mine and does not do them will be like a foolish man who built his house on the sand. And the rain fell, and the floods came, and the winds blew and beat against that**

house, and it fell, and great was the fall of it."

We build our foundation on Jesus Christ by first recognizing who He is and what He did for us on the cross. We then need to be talking to Him (praying) and listening to Him (reading His Word). Our foundation needs to be continually built and maintained:
1. Attending the gatherings on Saturday or Sunday.
2. Joining a Growth Community.
3. Creating a circle of friends that will build us up.

The devil does not want me to write a devotion. He is going to try everything to discourage me. We need to put on our Armor of God. Every morning we need to do this. Ephesians 6:11 says, **"Put on the whole armor of God, that you may be able to stand against the schemes of the devil."** I am going to make sure I am better at this. I need the Lord's armor every day to fight the demons of this world.

After thinking about this devotion and praying about it, the Lord gave me the verses I feel He wanted me to share with you. The Lord has worked in me, and I have learned a lot from writing this devotion. I need to be in the Word more and putting on my armor every day to keep the devil and his demons away.

> 1 Peter 5:8 says, *"Be sober-minded; be watchful. Your adversary the devil prowls around like a roaring lion, seeking someone to devour."*
>
> James 4:7 continues, *"Submit yourselves therefore to God. Resist the devil, and he will flee from you."*
>
> Finally, 2 Corinthians 11:14 says, *"And no wonder, for even Satan disguises himself as an angel of light."*

04 / *PASTOR CALEB COMBS, GATHERING PASTOR*

HIS
PREACHERS

I have heard it said that the key to making right choices, is the company you keep. The phrase, "Right voices equal right choices" rings so prominently in our lives. It is so important as followers of Christ that we put the right influencers who speak truth and wisdom into our lives. Whether that is the media we take in on a daily basis or the best friend who we confide our deepest secrets to, it is crucial that we let godly people speak truth into our lives.

1 Peter 5:8 is so clear that we need to be on guard and watchful because the devil is stalking us and actively trying to destroy our lives in any way possible. 1 Corinthians tells us that **"Bad company corrupts good morals."** However, the Bible is also clear that there is safety in the multitude of counsel. So, we cannot live and die with our own opinions and views. How do you decipher if something or someone is a good or bad influence in your life? Throughout this lesson, we will discuss how the devil uses "preachers/messengers" to influence us every day. I know, you were hoping I would give you a list of "preachers" who I classify as false teachers and hammer them throughout this lesson. However, my goal is to equip you with biblical and practical knowledge; so that, you can discern who should be speaking into your life, whether that is a preacher or a friend at work. What and who we are letting speak into our lives is crucial to our walk with Christ.

What or who is a good influencer in your life? _____

_____

_____

What or who is a bad influencer in your life? _____

_____

_____

When looking to God's Word, one story, in particular, stands out to me about a man who listened to the wrong voices and made the wrong choices. He had the right people talking to him but just would not listen to them. The man I am speaking about is Lot.

> Genesis 12:1-5a *"Now the Lord said to Abram, 'Go from your country and your kindred and your father's house to the land that I will show you. And I will make of you a great nation, and I will bless you and make your name great, so that you will be a blessing. I will bless those who bless you, and him who dishonors you I will curse, and in you all the families of the earth shall be blessed.' So Abram went, as the Lord had told him, and Lot went with him."*

Who was Lot to Abraham? (hint: keep reading in chapter 12)
_____
_____
_____

How would you feel about God making this promise to you and your family? _____
_____
_____

> Galatians 3:29
> *"And if you are Christ's, then you are Abraham's offspring, heirs according to promise."*

The Bible tells us that Abraham and Lot went on many journeys together and God blessed them abundantly. They were rich with many livestock, silver, and gold. God told Abraham to go, and He would lead him and his family. So, Abraham traveled through many cities and lands seeking where God would have him. There arose a conflict between Abraham and Lot, so they had to separate all that they owned. Abraham gave Lot the choice and Lot chose to move him and his family in the valley facing the evil city Sodom.

FUN FACT: When the Bible uses the term "valley" it commonly references not only a low spot geographically but also spiritually. The Psalmist references "walking through the valley of the shadow of death" yet God walks with him and comforts him. I am not sure if you are reading this from the valley, but one thing you can always cling to is the fact that Jesus will be with you on the highest mountain top or the lowest valley. All we need to do is call out to Him.

What do you think the conflict was between Abraham and Lot in Genesis 13? _____
_____
_____

What was wrong with Sodom? How do you think this influenced Lot and his family? _____
_____
_____

Lot ended up moving his family into the city of Sodom and participating in the evil that occurred in the city. Reading through Genesis Chapter 19 we see the depravity of this city and God ultimately attempting to save Lot and his family from the destruction of the city. Chaos and suffering came to not only Lot's immediate family, but generations to follow because Lot let the influence of the world destroy his family. All of this could have been avoided if Lot had not separated himself and his family from godly influences.

His Preachers

How could Lot have put better influencers around him? How about yourself? _____
_____
_____
_____

"Trust that God will put the right people in your life at the right time for the right reasons." Unknown

Four questions to ask about your influencer to find out if they are a GOOD or BAD influence:

1. Are they biblical? Does the advice and message you receive agree with what the Bible teaches or does it conflict with God's Word?
_____
_____
_____
_____

> Proverbs 12:26
> *"The righteous is a guide to his neighbor, but the way of the wicked leads them astray."*

2. Are they truthful? You need to hear things that do not make you feel good and might even hurt, but it is the truth. Sometimes the truth hurts, but we can take it, examine ourselves, and let our influencer push us to be better. _____
_____
_____
_____

> Proverbs 27:6
> *"Faithful are the wounds of a friend, but deceitful are the kisses of an enemy."*
>
> 2 Timothy 4: 3-4
> *"For the time is coming when people will not endure sound teaching, but having itching ears they will accumulate for themselves teachers to suit their own passions, and will turn away from listening to the truth and wander off into myths."*

3. Are they wise? Is the person you are letting speak into your life a wise person, or are they a fool and will lead you astray by the message they give you? _____

_____

_____

_____

_____

> Proverbs 13:20
> *"He who walks with wise men will be wise, But the companion of fools will suffer harm."*

4. Are they encouraging? Are they building you up or tearing you down? We are called to encourage each other and push each other to do good works. _____

_____

_____

> Hebrews 3:13
> *"But encourage one another daily, as long as it is called 'Today,' so that none of you may be hardened by sin's deceitfulness."*

As we close, we must examine who we let speak into our lives. Lot let the enemy use the world to express themselves and influence him and his family, which ultimately destroyed him. God has placed people around us who can "preach" wisdom and biblical knowledge into our daily lives, and we must use it. Use these questions to see if you are letting the enemy's "preachers" speak false doctrines and foolishness into your life. If you are in need of a positive and godly influence, stop by your church and ask a Pastor if he could connect you with someone who could mentor you. IT IS CRUCIAL to walk in godly council every day of our lives.

> Psalm 1:1
> *"How blessed is the man who does not walk in the counsel of the ungodly, nor stand in the path of sinners, nor sit in the seat of scoffers."*

His Preachers / Devotion 1

KNOW THE BOOK

Kyle Wendel / *Children & Student's Director*

> *"But false prophets also arose among the people, just as there will be false teachers among you, who will secretly bring in destructive heresies, even denying the Master who bought them, bringing upon themselves swift destruction. And many will follow their sensuality, and because of them the way of truth will be blasphemed. And in their greed they will exploit you with false words. Their condemnation from long ago is not idle, and their destruction is not asleep."* - 2 Peter 2:1-3

False teachers are very real. The Bible explicitly warns multiple times that there will be people that teach things that are far from the truth. The sad thing is many people will follow these false teachers because they are often great speakers and great with their words. I want to warn you today of false teachers. They are everywhere in our culture. They are there for a reason; they are there to keep others from the truth of the Gospel. False teachers come in all different shapes and sizes. Some may be the people you see on TV; some may be celebrities, some may be pastors or some someone else you know. Many false teachers even use the identity of a godly teacher for greed. The Bible clearly is warning us about these people for a reason. The truth will be blasphemed from these, and we need to be very careful of this trap.

> 1 Peter 5:8 says, *"Be sober-minded; be watchful. Your adversary the devil prowls around like a roaring lion, seeking someone to devour."*

You need to protect yourself from such things. It is easy to fall victim to false teachings because often they are great at teaching and speaking but because it is also accepted by most. The thing is the devil is looking for someone to take as prey just as a lion looks for prey. The Bible warns us to be sober-minded and watchful. We need to always be on guard with what we listen to and allow in our lives.

I would even tell you to check your pastors. If I am preaching to you, I would want you to make sure everything I say lines up with what the Word of God says. Don't just take your pastors word for everything. Yes, I believe you should trust your pastor but make sure for yourself that we are preaching what the Bible says. I encourage you to test any teaching that you put yourself under to see if it is in Scripture. The sad truth is there are a lot of preachers that twist the Gospel. Many preach a prosperity Gospel, which teaches that when you come to Christ your life will become great and you will be rich. Some preach that Jesus is not the only way to Heaven. There are many examples I could give you, but ultimately you need to make sure what we say is what the Bible teaches. Jesus tells us that He is the only way to God. There is no one and nothing else. He also does not say following Him will be all flowers and butterflies; He tells us to take up our cross and follow Him.

One last thing, I encourage you to guard others against false teachings as well. Do not let your family, friends, and people you know fall victim to the false teachings of this world. But rather find the truth in God's Word. The Bible is warning us of this threat so that we know it is there and to not ignore it.

His Preachers / Devotion 2

"O BE CAREFUL LITTLE..."

Phil Piasecki / *Worship Leader*

The age of social media has changed the way that we live our lives. We can stay in contact with people that we previously would not have been able to. If I wanted to, I could know what every person I graduated high school with is currently doing with their lives. I can get information on anything that I want in an instant on Twitter, and read every single person's reactions to that news. While there are many benefits to the internet and social media, there are also many downfalls. Social media and the internet have given people a platform to spread their beliefs that they previously never had access. This can be used in incredible ways, but also can be very destructive. These platforms give a more profound voice to the thoughts and teachings of false teachers that the devil is using today. Because of this increased exposure, Christians need to be even more diligent in guarding against these attacks of the devil. The appearance of false teachers should not surprise us; Scripture is very clear in warning us against them:

> *"For false christs and false prophets will arise and perform signs and wonders, to lead astray, if possible, the elect. But be on guard; I have told you all things beforehand."* Mark 13:22-23

> *"But false prophets also arose among the people, just as there will be false teachers among you, who will secretly bring in destructive heresies, even denying the Master who bought them, bringing upon themselves swift destruction."* 2 Peter 2:1

> *"For the time is coming when people will not endure sound teaching, but having itching ears they will accumulate for themselves teachers to suit their own passions, and will turn away from listening to the truth and wander off into myths. As for you, always be sober-minded, endure suffering, do the work of an evangelist, fulfill your ministry."* 2 Timothy 4:3-5

These Scriptures show us very clear warnings that false teachers are going to arise and preach destructive doctrine. The devil uses these preachers to attempt to lead believers astray from the true Gospel of Jesus Christ. Timothy warns us that people are going to want to be taught things that they want to hear, instead of things that they need to understand. It is our responsibility as believers to prepare ourselves to recognize false teaching and guard ourselves against it. One way to protect against false teaching is to make sure you are spending regular time in God's Word, asking God that He would help you discern what is being taught. The more we know the truth of the Bible, the easier it is for us to recognize when someone is teaching a false doctrine. God has given us His Word, and He has given us His Holy Spirit for discernment to identify false teaching. Daily we are exposed to teaching that is contrary to what God's Word teaches us. If we do not know what the Bible says then we will have no way of knowing what is true and what is false. We need to make the Word of God a priority in our lives, and when we do that, we will be able to spot a false teacher from miles away.

His Preachers / Devotion 3

TRANSFORMED

Pastor Ryan Story / *Student Pastor*

I remember when I first got a Walkman. If I am not mistaken, I was about 11 years old. I walked up to the old Harmony House in Waterford and bought two cassettes. Now I had gotten cassette tapes as gifts in the past, but this was the first time I bought my own. The first two cassette tapes I ever purchased were the soundtracks to Batman Forever and Dangerous Minds. Do not judge. In 1995, Seal's "Kiss From a Rose" and Coolio's "Gangster Paradise" where and still are the greatest songs ever. I remember getting back home, and my parents asked where I was, and I told them. I do not recall the exact conversation, but I remember getting my Coolio cassette taken away because my parents deemed it inappropriate. Looking back on it, I can see that them wanting to keep certain influences away from their children was the right call; however, I do have those entire songs memorized to this day. Now, I am not trying to degrade the hip-hop culture or even take shots at rap music, but I often catch myself realizing how much influence media of all types has on my life. While in my day it was the hip-hop revolution that took place, I am pretty sure when 1980 hair bands or The Beatles became popular young people were influenced as well.

I am not a legalist when it comes to movies, television, video games, or music. I have my lines that I will not cross when it comes to what I deem viewable. I also do not always think that "the devil controls Hollywood," but I do believe that there are some very anti-Jesus sentiments out there. I love movies. In high school, I use to listen to all types of music from country to rock to rap. And be honest, who does not love watching prime time sitcoms, as I write this I have "Friends" playing on Netflix. We all have our media vices. With all of that being said, the truth is the things we watch or listen to, do in fact influence us. This is a fact we cannot deny. Sadly, we often run toward our entertainment vices instead of running to better our walk with Christ.

We could talk all day about how the devil is out to destroy our lives, but I do not think that he always uses such aggressive tactics. Sometimes all he has to do is get us to not read our Bible, or to skip Church because of a football game, or to skip a Growth Community because there is a band in town. Again none of those activities is necessarily sinning, but if we are not careful, we start being influenced by worldly entertainment. At times I feel we have all failed to live up to Paul's warning in Romans 12:2, **"Do not be conformed to this world."** If you are going to brush me off and say "I can watch football and still be a Christian," I totally agree. Paul says in the second part of Romans 12:2, **"But be transformed."** Be honest if you are listening to music you should not, or watching movies or television that you should not, into what are you being transformed? The devil does not want us to transform into what Jesus wants us to become, he wants us to conform to the world. Sometime this week turn off the TV and open your Bible, read it with your family. Take an honest look at the shows you and your children watch. How do they help you with growing in your prayer life? Take a second to look at the songs on your Spotify, how godly are they? There are seasons in our life where we have to remove certain vices and focus on growing our relationship with Jesus. It scares me to think how many Christians the devil has tricked into a lukewarm lifestyle with just music preferences.

His Preachers / Devotion 4

HOLE IN ONE

Josh Lahring / *Production Director*

I have never been one to play any sports, but over the past year I have taken up golf. I do not know much about it other than the goal is to try and get the ball in the hole in the least amount of strokes. I know there are a ton of rules, but I have no idea what they are. Someone could tell me anything about the rules, and I would probably believe them. I have never taken any time to read or learn anything about the sport.

In many ways, as Christians, we do the same thing. We just try to 'play the game.' We do not take the time to know our book, the Bible. We just listen to whoever sounds good to us. This is a danger, and it can be easy to fall into false teachings.

2 Timothy 4:3-5 warns and challenges us, *"For the time is coming when people will not endure sound teaching, but having itching ears they will accumulate for themselves teachers to suit their own passions, and will turn away from listening to the truth and wander off into myths. As for you, always be sober-minded, endure suffering, do the work of an evangelist, fulfill your ministry."*

For many people, they just want to hear a comforting motivational speech. They want to hear how good they are, that God loves them and that He is going to bless them. They do not want the truth. Their ears 'itch' for someone to make them feel good.

The Bible should not be just a rule book to us; it is our way to know God and let Him speak truth into our lives. He loves us and has a plan for our lives. It might challenge us, convict us, and even push us out of our comfort zone. Jesus was radical in His teaching. Unfortunately, to many the things that they heard did not sound right to them. They looked for someone who might sound really good to them.

Paul writes in Acts 17:11, **"Now these Jews were more noble than those in Thessalonica; they received the word with all eagerness, examining the Scriptures daily to see if these things were so."** The Bereans listened to Paul and still re-examined the Bible to make sure he was telling the truth. They trusted God's Word and evaluated everyone else based on that.

If we do not know the Word of God, we will not know whether what we are hearing is truth or not.

Study the Bible.

Get involved in a growth community.

His Preachers / Devotion 5

FALSE TEACHERS

Roger Allen / *Facilities Director*

"*Do your best to present yourself to God as one approved, a worker who has no need to be ashamed, rightly handling the word of truth*" (2 Timothy 2:15).

In the last few years, a couple of high-profile pastors have been forced to leave the ministries they started. Whether they stepped down or were removed, there is one thing that resonates, that sadly their fall took many unsuspecting people with them. This did not happen overnight. According to the Bible, they had disqualified themselves long before it was played out in public. They were consumed with themselves and deliberately blurred the lines between biblical truths and falsehoods. Something new, exciting, and different can divert our attention from the truth. Someone who has been given the gift of speech can lead us in a direction that has dire consequences. The sheep are scattered. Why were the warning signs ignored? The Bible tells us that even the elect can be fooled. Like a cat to a laser light, we love our ears tickled. Matthew 24:24 says, **"For false christs and false prophets will arise and perform great signs and wonders, so as to lead astray, if possible even the elect."** Beware of the wolf in sheep's clothing!

Did they lose sight of their pastoral responsibilities? Were they diligent with their heart? Did they give into a culture that thought unpopular biblical principles were obsolete or were they deceived? One thing for sure, with so much at stake we should be diligent in our pursuit of the Word. Jesus has given us the Bible as our litmus test to weigh the measure of the leader under whom we sit. We have a responsibility to discern what is right and honorable from that, which is evil. 1 Thessalonians 5:21 adds, **"But test everything; hold fast what is good."**

His Preachers / Devotion 6

FALLING STAR WARS

Noble Baird / *Community Center Director*

For as long as I can remember, I have always loved reading and watching movies about mythical worlds. Whether it be: *Star Wars, Lord of the Rings, Harry Potter, Narnia, or Wizard of OZ*, I love being able to dive into these fun and imaginary worlds. Now, before I get started, know that I do not condone or support magic or witchcraft. That being said, one of the greatest antagonists I have ever seen was Voldemort from Harry Potter. As the story unfolds, Voldemort recruits a group of followers called the Death Eaters. These Death Eaters continually attack and plot against Harry and his friends, doing all they can to stop the young wizards. Their goal is to recruit more followers to Voldemort's cause of becoming the most powerful wizard of all time.

In 2 Peter 2:1-3, Peter writes, **"But false prophets also arose among the people, just as there will be false teachers among you, who will secretly bring in destructive heresies, even denying the Master who bought them, bringing upon themselves swift destruction. And many will follow their sensuality, and because of them the way of truth will be blasphemed. And in their greed they will exploit you with false words. Their condemnation from long ago is not idle, and their destruction is not asleep."** Peter lays it all out for us when he writes here about the reality of the false teachers and prophets that were coming out of the woodwork. Their goal is simple, to give false testimony and preach false teachings that contradict Christ; or as Peter writes the Master.

The Death Eaters gave their allegiance to Voldemort and his mission. They travel all over the world trying to destroy innocent wizards and trying to convince the people that Voldemort is the one whom they need to follow. Likewise, Satan has recruited hundreds of false teachers and preachers to aid him in his mission of devouring and destroying the lives of everyone in this world. These preachers will not stop at anything and will take on any means necessary to carry out Satan's mission. Therefore, as followers of Christ, we must be watchful of these false preachers. In 1 John 4:1-3, John writes,

> *"Beloved, do not believe every spirit, but test the spirits to see whether they are from God, for many false prophets have gone out into the world. By this you know the Spirit of God: every spirit that confesses that Jesus Christ has come in the flesh is from God, and every spirit that does not confess Jesus is not from God. This is the spirit of the antichrist, which you heard was coming and now is in the world already."*

So, this is the challenge I want to leave with you this week; be careful. John told us how we must test the false teachers and preachers that are already in this world. He did not say they might come, or they were eventually on their way, but that they are already here. Just as the Death Eaters were walking amongst the people, disguised in the schools, and attacking Harry and his friends; so do these false preachers walk amongst us. They are in the workplace, the schools, on TV, they write books, and even preach in the church, with the mission to deceive as many from the cause of Christ as they can. So, be careful and watchful for these false preachers, because they are very real and they will do whatever it takes to sway the world from Christ.

05 / *PASTOR TREVOR COLE*

HIS END

His End

Our lives here on earth are filled with moments of happiness. Our lives are also filled with moments of hurt and pain. For much of my life I was blessed enough not to have to face the loss of a loved one. I remember being in my first year of college and hearing that my grandfather had passed away. At that moment, all of the memories of my relationship with him flashed through my mind, and I now understood what it meant to lose someone close to me. Unfortunately, as we get older, we will face more and more of those experiences.

Who did you start thinking about as you read that paragraph?
_____
_____
_____

It is not just losing loved ones either. We will face all kinds of hurt from those around us and what we have caused ourselves. We can trace it all to one moment in history.

> Genesis 3:6 *"So when the woman saw that the tree was good for food, and that it was a delight to the eyes, and that the tree was to be desired to make one wise, she took of its fruit and ate, and she also gave some to her husband who was with her, and he ate."*
>
> Ephesians 2:1-2 reminds us, *"And you were dead in the trespasses and sins in which you once walked, following the course of this world, following the prince of the power of the air, the spirit that is now at work in the sons of disobedience."*

Adam and Eve gave into the temptation of the devil and rejected the one command God gave them. But we cannot put the blame on them, had we been there, we would have all made the same choice.

As Ephesians 2:1-2 remind us, we all have a sin nature, and now the world is broken by it. Whenever I talk to people about facing difficult circumstances in life, the most common question is "why would God let this happen to that person or me?"

Take a moment and reflect on the most difficult experience in your life so far. _____
_____
_____
_____

Have you ever had a moment where you asked God "why would you let this happen?" Describe that moment. _____
_____
_____

In today's study I just want to give you two pieces of encouragement.

> Romans 11:33 *"Oh, the depth of the riches and wisdom and knowledge of God! How unsearchable are his judgments and how inscrutable his ways!"*

First of all, stop trying to answer the question "why would God let this happen?" When you are facing something painful, it is wise to ask "is this happening because of something I did?" Sometimes we are the cause of the pain in our life. Our anger, greed, lies, pride, and so many others often cause us some serious difficulties, and we need to make sure that we ask God's forgiveness and strength to overcome. The problem arises when we direct our hurt and pain at God and question His plan. The truth is that this side of eternity, we may never understand why God allows certain things into our life. We are better off telling God that we trust Him no matter what and plead for His strength to face the pain in front of us.

His End

Verses like Romans 11:33 remind me just how futile it is for me to try to comprehend what God might be doing. We will find so much more comfort and peace by simply trusting in the depth of His wisdom and His ability to take a broken world and make something truly beautiful out of it.

Describe a time when you stood in awe of God's wisdom.
_____
_____
_____

If we begin to make a sort of mental catalog of the times we saw God's perfect plan in our lives and the lives of others, it will help us trust Him when things get tough.

Second, if you have put your faith in Jesus for the forgiveness of your sin, there is coming a day when the devil's reign on this earth will end.

> Genesis 3:14-15 *"The Lord God said to the serpent, 'Because you have done this, cursed are you above all livestock and above all beasts of the field; on your belly you shall go, and dust you shall eat all the days of your life. I will put enmity between you and the woman, and between your offspring and her offspring; he shall bruise your head, and you shall bruise his heel.'"*

I know the wording can be a bit confusing, but what is this verse referring to when it says "you shall bruise his heel?" *Jesus*
_____
_____
_____

What about when it says "he shall bruise your head?"

_____

_____

_____

> Revelation 20:10 *"And the devil who had deceived them was thrown into the lake of fire and sulfur where the beast and the false prophet were, and they will be tormented day and night forever and ever."*

The second piece of encouragement I want to give you is, if you have put your faith in Jesus for the forgiveness of your sin, there is coming a day when the devil's reign on this earth will end. While on earth we will constantly face the roaring lion who is seeking to devour us, but God promises us that his end is coming.

I enjoy the outdoors. That does not mean I am some back country tough guy, but I like to get out and hike and read the occasional outdoor magazine. Recently, I read about this crazy piece of equipment that hikers and skiers in high avalanche risk areas use called an avalanche airbag. If you were wearing this when an avalanche hit, you simply pull a handle on the backpack, and it inflates a sort of bubble to keep you protected along with a breathing tube, so you have enough fresh air when the snow surrounds you. I have got to imagine that wearing this would give you so much comfort in those high-risk areas! You might get buried, but you should be protected for long enough to have someone rescue you. Amazing. When the pain and discouragement of this world seem to come crashing down like an avalanche, threatening to squeeze the joy from your life, remember that God alone can protect you and that it will not always be this way. Hope in Him.

His End / Devotion 1

SATAN'S END

Debbie Gabbara / Assistant to the Gathering Pastor

"Now war arose in heaven, Michael and his angels fighting against the dragon. And the dragon and his angels fought back, but he was defeated, and there was no longer any place for them in heaven. And the great dragon was thrown down, that ancient serpent, who is called the devil and Satan, the deceiver of the whole world — he was thrown down to the earth, and his angels were thrown down with him." Revelation 12:7-9

"But woe to you, O earth and sea, for the devil has come down to you in great wrath, because he knows that his time is short!" Revelation 12:12b

"…and the devil who had deceived them was thrown into the lake of fire and sulfur where the beast and the false prophet were, and they will be tormented day and night forever and ever." Revelation 20:10

It is not a question or something that we can debate; we all know that one day we will leave this world. The problem in every mind is "where will we go?"

The Bible is very clear in telling us that when our time on earth is done, we will continue to live forever. Whether we live forever in Heaven with God the Father or in Hell separated forever from God, is a decision we must make while we are here. Our days are short. We must make a choice to choose Jesus as our Lord and Savior, so that we may join Him in Heaven forever. If we do not choose Jesus, then we have rejected Him, and the Bible says that the penalty is to be separated from God forever in Hell. We must make sure that our name is written in the Lamb's Book of Life and secure our eternity in Heaven with God.

Satan, the angel called Lucifer, has waged war against God. Satan knows the Bible, and he knows his days are short.

My brother-in-law works for the Oakland County Sheriff's Department. I was thinking about situations that he has been in when a gunman is barricaded in a building. The outcome is inevitable. Either the gunman will surrender, be arrested, and go to jail, or at times when the situation escalates, and gunfire begins, the gunman's great standoff very often ends in his death. Yet, in his pride and anger, the gunman somehow convinces himself that he can control the situation and manipulate another outcome.

Satan knows the Bible very well. He quoted Scripture to Jesus when he tempted Him on the mountain. Somehow, in his pride and anger, he chooses to wage war against God and all of Heaven. He must know that his fate has already been sealed and his final sentence is to be cast into the Lake of Fire, where there will be torment night and day forever. Hell was created for Satan and his demons. Unfortunately, all of those who do not choose to have a personal relationship with Jesus will be there with them.

Satan knows the end is coming. We are on a timetable, too. Psalm 139 tells us that God knows the number of our days. Our days were planned in advance for us before we were ever formed. Do not let your day slip by without choosing life, choosing Jesus. Do not fight the fight of pride and anger along with Satan. The Bible tells us that God wants to give us life, abundant life, not just now, but forever in Heaven with Him.

We are created with free will. According to the Scriptures in Revelation 12, the angels must have been created with free will as well. I try to imagine what it would have been like to have been set up as an angel, living in Heaven with God, surrounded by His beauty and holiness. There is no sin and life is perfect. My brain struggles to comprehend it. So, I definitely cannot imagine how Lucifer (aka Satan, the devil) could think that he could be as God. I also cannot imagine, knowing that our end is inevitable, Heaven or Hell, why everyone would not choose Jesus. Have you made your choice?

> *"Be sober-minded; be watchful. Your adversary the devil prowls around like a roaring lion, seeking someone to devour."* 1 Peter 5:8

> *"For the wages of sin is death, but the free gift of God is eternal life in Christ Jesus our Lord."* Romans 6:23

His End / Devotion 2

THE BUBBLE

Phil Piascoki / *Worship Leader*

The invention of the DVR has revolutionized how live sporting events are watched. Someone can miss looking at a game live, DVR it, and watch it later as if they did not miss anything. The trick to doing this is staying in what is called "The Bubble." Staying in The Bubble means not finding out any details about a sporting event so that everything that happens in the game is a surprise. I will never forget the day when my dad mentioned the final score of a Michigan vs. Michigan State football game to a random guy standing next to us. The guy was in "The Bubble" and was furious when my dad told him the outcome of the game. If you have ever watched a recorded sporting event with already knowing your team wins, you know how different the experience is. When your team is losing for parts of it, there is no anxiety; you already know the outcome. In comparison, we are not in "the bubble" in our Christian life. We have the book of Revelation, and we know how the battle of Good vs. Evil ends. Look what Revelation 20 says about it:

> *"Then I saw an angel coming down from heaven, holding in his hand the key to the bottomless pit and a great chain. And he seized the dragon, that ancient serpent, who is the devil and Satan, and bound him for a thousand years, and threw him into the pit, and shut it and sealed it over him, so that he might not deceive the nations any longer, until the thousand years were ended. After that he must be released for a little while"* (Revelation 20:1-3).

> *"And when the thousand years are ended, Satan will be released from his prison and will come out to deceive the*

> *nations that are at the four corners of the earth, Gog and Magog, to gather them for battle; their number is like the sand of the sea. And they marched up over the broad plain of the earth and surrounded the camp of the saints and the beloved city, but fire came down from heaven and consumed them, and the devil who had deceived them was thrown into the lake of fire and sulfur where the beast and the false prophet were, and they will be tormented day and night forever and ever"* (Revelation 20:7-10).

These verses paint an incredible picture of what the final battle between God and Satan is going to look like. This fight ends with Satan being thrown into Hell (actually The Lake of Fire) to suffer for eternity, along with beasts and false prophets. The Christian life can be difficult, and the world can seem hopeless at times, but we can take solace in the fact that we know who ultimately wins.

> *"Therefore God has highly exalted him and bestowed on him the name that is above every name, so that at the name of Jesus every knee should bow, in heaven and on earth and under the earth, and every tongue confess that Jesus Christ is Lord, to the glory of God the Father"* (Philippians 2:9-11).

One day, literally every living thing is going to proclaim that Jesus Christ is Lord. Christ will be seated on His throne and will rule forever. We have an incredible eternity in the presence of Jesus Christ to look forward to as believers. An eternity of being able to worship God through our every action, being sinless, and having every inch of us reflect the glory of God. If you find yourself discouraged, let this incredible reality be an encouragement. There will be a day when there is no more pain, sickness, or death. Christ will have perfected everything as He originally intended it to be in the Garden. Satan will try to defeat Christ, he will fail, and God will forever be glorified.

His End / Devotion 3

THE END

Pastor Ryan Story / Student Pastor

Hiroo Onoda was a Japanese soldier who continued fighting World War II a full 29 years after the Japanese surrendered because he did not know the war was over. In 1944, Onoda was sent to Lubang Island in the Philippines. His orders were simple: "You are absolutely forbidden to die by your own hand. It may take three years, it may take five, but whatever happens, we'll come back for you. Until then, so long as you have one soldier, you are to continue to lead him. You may have to live on coconuts. If that is the case, live on coconuts! Under no circumstances are you to give up your life voluntarily." On March 10th, 1975, Onoda was found and surrendered his sword to the Pilipino government. Despite fighting and killing people after World War II ended, Onoda was still hailed as a hero in his return to Japan.

The scariest adversary is one that does not know they are defeated. Onoda was willing to stay loyal to the cause and never give up, despite the fact the war had already been won. I often encounter students who ask me, "Why is life so hard despite the fact that they live for Jesus?" One of the only answers I can ever think of is the fact that Satan knows he is defeated, he knows he lost, he knows his final resting place. I do not imagine "the roaring lion" taking this loss well. The devil is a frantic sore loser who wants to take everyone down in his path. Since Jesus has set us all free from the devil's grasps, we should expect adversity, trials, and tribulation.

I am a huge strategy game fan. Any game where you have to get into someone's head to win is an instant favorite in my book. The Bible is clear in several areas about what Satan does. There is never a moment where the Bible is not clear about how he is here to attempt to bring us down. Now I know that when the devil swings and it connects it hurts. I have seen great Christians brought down and broken because of sin and temptations. 2 Corinthians 2:11 says, **"So that we would not be outwitted by Satan; for we are not ignorant of his designs."** Let us all understand that he is out to get us, let us not be ignorant of that. Be on guard, but if we know there is an enemy that is never going to give up trying to destroy us, who will be relentless, who will attack us in the most horrific ways at times, let us remind the devil that because of Jesus and what He did on the cross we shall never be outwitted or ignorant of his designs. I love the NIV translation on this verse because instead of designs it says schemes. The devil is a roaring, sore loser who wants to ruin anyone's life that he can before his end is met.

An adversary who does not know he lost can only win, if we let him. Too often in life, we focus more on the schemes and less on the gift of salvation and the victory that brings us. We all wake-up and fail in our walk with God. We all stumble. Losing a battle is one thing. Do not give up on fighting the war because of one bad day. That is exactly what a losing enemy wants out of you. An enemy that does not know he has lost is scary, but a victor who refuses to give up is stronger.

His End / Devotion 4

DING DONG THE WITCH IS DEAD AND ROSEBUD WAS HIS SLED

Ken Perry / *Assistant to the Reach Pastor*

Spoiler alert! I cannot stand those words. They mean that some long-awaited outcome is about to be revealed and if you do not want to know how it turned out, you had better walk away, close your ears, or turn the channel. It happens all the time with movies. If you do not catch the opening night, you run the risk of knowing how the movie ends just by walking down the street. It happens all the time with sports. I know of many guys who record an event only to be "alerted" by the text of a well-meaning friend or they receive an update because they forgot to turn off the notifications tab on the news feed. I have told myself never to be that guy. Never be the guy that spoils the outcome for someone else. With that said, I still feel compelled to tell you the ending to the best-selling book in history…The Bible says that Satan gets defeated in the end!

To make a great book, you need a protagonist (the main character) and an antagonist (the main character's chief adversary or opponent). Satan has been God's antagonist from the very beginning. The Bible is not just history, it is His Story, and in Genesis 3 we see his start. Genesis 3:1 records the fall of man and guess who is there? You got it, Satan himself in the guise of a serpent, **"Now the serpent was more crafty than any other beast of the field that the Lord God had made."**

We know he was created, and we also know his purpose. 1 Peter 5:8 tells us, **"Be sober-minded; be watchful. Your adversary <u>the devil prowls around like a roaring lion, seeking someone to devour.</u>"** His only purpose is to either keep you from accepting the

Lord as your Savior or to draw you away from the relationship you already enjoy with Christ Jesus. What we sometimes gloss over, or forget in the midst of trials, is that Satan loses in the end. Do not be deceived or dismayed brothers and sisters, he gets what is coming to him. I am a guy that likes to see justice meted out immediately. When the person speeds by at 90 mph, I want to see the red lights of Michigan's finest close behind. When someone breaks the law, I want to see them in handcuffs soon after. I think we all want to see the bad guy get his due. Thankfully, the God of all justice, the judge over all, the great I AM will bring the final judgment to Satan. Revelation 20:10 says, **"And the devil who had deceived them was thrown into the lake of fire and sulfur were the beast and the great prophet were, and they will be tormented day and night forever and ever."**

Is that not great news? The Bible tells us that Satan is the god (little g) of this world but according to John 16:33 we are to take heart because Jesus overcame the world. We get to go into our battles, our struggles, our chaos at work, our minefield of the family. We get to go into everything fighting FROM victory not FOR victory. Those two words, from and for, make all the difference in the world do they not? Jesus already won the battle; it was finished in the completed work of Christ on the cross of Calvary. Please remember that the next time you are faced with something that seems too tough to handle. Remember we have a God in Heaven that has gone through everything with which we are tempted and struggle. Remember Hebrews 4:15, **"For we do not have a high priest who is unable to sympathize with our weaknesses, but one who in every respect has been tempted as we are, yet without sin."**

God is victorious, Satan is defeated, and those who call on the name of Jesus get to walk in newness of life knowing the outcome of the greatest story ever told. There is great confidence in that knowledge my friends. Have an amazing day!

His End / Devotion 5

NOT TODAY SATAN

Shawna Johnson

If you have been around me for any length of time, I would almost guarantee you have heard me sing the old hymn "Victory in Jesus."

O victory in Jesus,
My Savior, forever.
He sought me and bought me
With His redeeming blood;
He loved me ere I knew Him
And all my love is due Him,
He plunged me to victory,
Beneath the cleansing flood.

It is my favorite! For almost everything in life I refer to the victory, we have in Him. It is just so exciting to me! There is one thing, however, of which we have to be aware. Though we have victory, we also have an enemy that continually tries to defeat us. I hate that part. I do not even want to give Satan the time of day. But he does exist, and he wants to steal, kill, and destroy the things of God (John 10:10).

I want to get one thing straight, just because I work at a Church does not mean I have it together all the time. I am so grateful for the opportunity to work in full-time ministry, but it does not make me a better believer or follower of Jesus than anyone else. That being said, the struggle has been real lately. God's Word does not tell us that when we accept Christ everything will be easy and we will never have struggles. It does, however, say we can stand firm when we face difficulty, and our main opponent, the devil. Ephesians 6:10-11 says, **"Finally, be strong in the Lord and in the strength of his**

might. Put on the whole armor of God, that you may be able to stand against the schemes of the devil." Did you hear that? We can stand against the schemes of the devil!

In the end, Satan will no longer be able to deceive and destroy God's people. Until then we stand firm in Christ, put on the whole armor of God, and let Him fight for us.

■ *"If God is for us, who can be against us?"* (Romans 8:31)

Not today Satan, not tomorrow, not ever.

His End / Devotion 6

LAKE OF FIRE

Noble Baird / *Community Center Director*

On December 17, 2003, *The Lord of the Rings: The Return of the King* was released in theaters all over the nation. Now, although it was almost three and a half hours long, it is in the top twenty all time grossing movies bringing in over 1.1 billion dollars. The story that J.R.R. Tolkien writes and Peter Jackson then took us on cinematically is, in my opinion, one of the greatest trilogies of all time. For those of you unfamiliar with *The Lord of the Rings* trilogy, it is a tale of a young hobbit and his friends who are taken on a journey to return a ring to the place it was created to be destroyed. The reason being is because this ring was made to rule the world, which then begins the battle between man and the one who created this ring, Sauron. Now, Sauron has one mission, to rule all of Middle Earth. His way of going about this was through the One Ring, which would be used to control the leaders across Middle Earth who wore the Rings of Power.

Over the last five weeks, we have talked about Satan, beginning with his fall and mission, all the way to now with his end. In Revelation 20:7-10, John writes,

> *"And when the thousand years are ended, Satan will be released from his prison and will come out to deceive the nations that are at the four corners of the earth, Gog and Magog, to gather them for battle; their number is like the sand of the sea. And they marched up over the broad plain of the earth and surrounded the camp of the saints and the beloved city, but fire came down from heaven and consumed them, and the devil who had deceived them was thrown into the lake of fire and sulfur where the beast and the false prophet were,*

■ *and they will be tormented day and night forever and ever."*

In this passage, John writes us the vision which he is given by God of Satan's end. Although his mission was to deceive the world and conquer over Christ, he loses. He is defeated and will ultimately be thrown into the lake of fire, where he will be in torment and suffer forever.

Sauron wages a great war on man. He deceives many, gains thousands to his cause. There is a great final battle which ensues at Minas Tirith and the Black Gate in Mordor. As the battle rages in Minas Tirith and the battle is about to begin at the Black Gate, Frodo destroys the One Ring. As the One Ring was destroyed, Sauron is crushed and defeated. In an instant, all of Sauron's followers and his army are defeated. They are swallowed up by the earth and fall just as he does. I love this imagery because it reminds me of what I imagine of Satan's defeat. In an instant, fire will rain down on Satan's followers and his "great" army, and they will be consumed. Then, Satan himself will be cast into the lake of fire; eternally separated from God and us, only to endure pain and suffering forever.

So as we wrap up this series on Satan, have hope. Remember that we have already won the great and final battle. When Jesus died, that veil was torn, and we are no longer separated from our Father. Yes, it is going to be tough, there will be trials, we will suffer, some have even given their lives fighting Satan's mission; however, have hope just as John tells us, we win!

OUR MISSION

Matthew 28:19-20: *"Go therefore and make disciples of all nations, baptizing them in the name of the Father and of the Son and of the Holy Spirit, teaching them to observe all that I have commanded you. And behold, I am with you always, to the end of the age."*

REACH

At The River Church, you will often hear the phrase, "we don't go to church, we are the Church." We believe that as God's people, our primary purpose and goal is to go out and make disciples of Jesus Christ. We encourage you to reach the world in your local communities.

GATHER

Weekend Gatherings at The River Church are all about Jesus, through singing, giving, serving, baptizing, taking the Lord's Supper, and participating in messages that are all about Jesus and bringing glory to Him. We know that when followers of Christ gather together in unity, it's not only a refresher it's bringing life-change.

GROW

Our Growth Communities are designed to mirror the early church in Acts as having "all things in common." They are smaller collections of believers who spend time together studying the word, knowing and caring for one another relationally, and learning to increase their commitment to Christ by holding one another accountable.

The River Church
8393 E. Holly Rd. Holly, MI 48442
theriverchurch.cc • info@theriverchurch.cc

BOOKS BY THE RIVER CHURCH

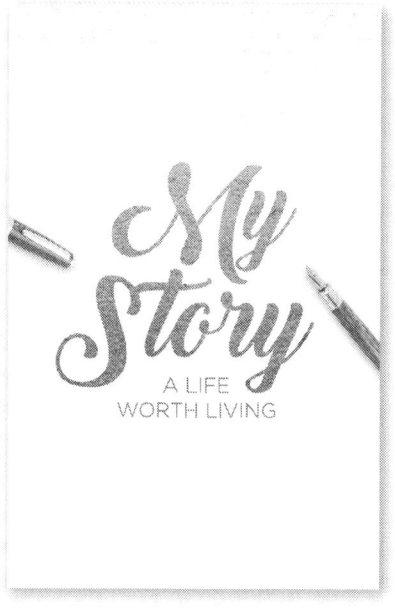

Buried
HOPE IN ALL CIRCUMSTANCES

A 5 WEEK STUDY GUIDE WITH DAILY DEVOTIONS

the Family Challenge
FINDING BALANCE IN A DEMANDING WORLD

My Story
A LIFE WORTH LIVING

What a Mess
A STUDY OF 1 CORINTHIANS

Made in the USA
San Bernardino, CA
13 August 2017